BRAVE AGAIN

Your Roadmap from Heartbreak to Happiness

ANNIE HUANG

First published by Busybird Publishing 2018
Copyright © 2018 Annie Huang

ISBN
Print: 978-1-925692-86-0
Ebook: 978-1-925692-87-7

Annie Huang has asserted her right under the Copyright, Designs and Patents Act 1988 to be identified as the author of this work. The information in this book is based on the author's experiences and opinions. The publisher specifically disclaims responsibility for any adverse consequences, which may result from use of the information contained herein. Permission to use information has been sought by the author. Any breaches will be rectified in further editions of the book.

Cover design: Busybird Publishing
Layout and typesetting: Busybird Publishing
Editor: Robert Frolla

Busybird Publishing
2/118 Para Road
Montmorency, Victoria
Australia 3094
www.busybird.com.au

Annie has truly helped me change my life! Her coaching has been so supportive, caring and insightful, I thoroughly look forward to every session. She has helped me achieve things I never thought possible. I am so grateful to have found her!

Skye Smith, Graphic Designer

I call Annie the 'motivator'! The energy during our time together carried me through the weeks of tough deadlines and stressful moments which then in turn resulted in achieving some amazing milestones. If you are looking for someone to hold you accountable to achieve your dreams in a focused, yet encouraging way, then Annie is the coach for you!

Kyla Neill, HR Consultant

Annie is an inspirational coach who helped me gain clarity in different areas of my life. During our sessions she was always present, focused and to the point. Her energy is very high which makes action-taking seem effortless.

Sabine Biesenberger, Online Business Strategist

Annie has helped me to recalibrate my internal GPS to take control of my life. She showed me how to work with my inner critic and to combat negative self-talk with kindness and acceptance, thus enabling me to grow as a person. Thank you Annie for all of your research and effort to create this program to help people on their own journey.

Jodi Fraser, Production Assistant

I really loved being part of Annie's coaching group. Her warmth and compassion for others is evident as soon as you join. I really feel that I am able to take control better over the direction that my life is heading in and I now feel I have the tools to do this more successfully.

Melissa Prendergast, Artist

This workshop has been the best investment in my life for a long time. I have seen psychologists over the years, but this day provided life-changing tools and strategies that I can implement now to live a much more peaceful life.

Louise Brighouse, Massage Therapist

To my family and friends for your love and support over the years.

Contents

Introduction: Picking up the Pieces

When one door closes, another opens; but we often look so long and so regretfully upon the closed door that we do not see the one that has opened for us.
– Alexander Graham Bell

Scars

They say that you should write from your scar, not your wound.

It's been nearly five years since my devastating breakup that led to so many things – including this book – and I am now looking back at my scar. It's not a fresh scar anymore, and on most days I don't even remember it's there. I have travelled a long way on my healing journey to be where I am now.

You might be in a lot of pain too right now. If you are reading this book, chances are you are probably going through a breakup, separation or divorce, and are struggling to get back on your feet.

Maybe you are overwhelmed by all the painful emotions that you can't even think straight. Or if you are a little further along and are no longer consumed by anger or despair, perhaps you are finding out that you are a stranger to yourself, having lost a lot of confidence and even your sense of self, and you can't see any hope for the future.

This book will give you what you are looking for: practical tools and strategies to help you get through the tough and uncertain days ahead, as well as gentle and loving reminders to help you soothe your pain and hopefully bring you some kind of solace.

I will also be sharing my personal journey through my own breakup and the valuable lessons I learned to help illustrate some of the ideas and tools in the book.

Whether you are at the brink of a breakup, are currently going through it or have already gone through it, you will find something useful here.

Two Choices

Many people believe that time heals all wounds. If that were the case, few of us would walk around with childhood wounds or other traumas that we experienced a long time ago. To varying degrees, we all have some healing work to do, and there is no better time than now. A breakup brings out our fears and reveals our beliefs and patterns so we can finally see them clearly.

Right now is a pivotal moment for change. What you do in the post-breakup period will have a profound effect on your healing journey. So don't leave it up to chance or wait for time to heal your wounds. Take an active part in your journey.

You have two choices now: you can either put all your wounds in a box and pretend everything is fine and go on with your life as if nothing had happened; or you can actively participate in your own healing to properly heal your wounds and start a new life with intention and purpose – a *conscious breakup*, as I call it. It's your choice.

This book is about the latter – using your breakup as the doorway to personal growth and fulfilment. I would like to show you how to do that by thinking, feeling and acting differently.

I love the saying, "if you always do what you've always done, you will always get what you've always got." So if you've had a few bad or even disastrous breakups in the past, I encourage you to be open-minded and try something different to have a different kind of healing journey – one that will lead to a stronger, happier you and an exciting new life.

My Story – Part I

Owning our story and loving ourselves through that process is the bravest thing that we'll ever do.
– Brené Brown

So who am I and why I am writing this book? The short answer is that I've had my heart really, really broken before and I managed to not only survive the heartbreak, but also used it as a doorway to transform my life, my career and my relationships. But that's a rather broad answer, so let me tell you my story.

I met my ex-boyfriend while I was on a backpacking trip through Central America. I had taken time off work and I was planning to travel all the way from Mexico to Panama. However, when I got to Guatemala – which was only my second stop – I met my ex. I fell head over heels for him and after dating him for only a month, I decided to quit my job and move from Australia to Guatemala to be with him.

All in one month!

In my defence, I felt like I had found 'the one' and all I wanted to do was to be with him 24/7, start a family and grow old together. I was utterly and hopelessly in love with him.

By the way, I thought this sort of thing didn't happen to people like me. I am someone who prides herself on being logical and rational, partly due to my upbringing and my education. I was brought up an atheist by parents who were strict and pragmatic. I was also a lawyer by profession before

I became a life coach. Even though I did have quite an unusual legal career, I was still very much a show-me-the-evidence, let's-examine-all-the-facts and analyse-everything-to-death kind of girl. It was so *not* me to throw caution to the wind and fall in love without reservations.

Fast forward two years, we were living in a shared apartment with a few other expats. We were very happy. Or at least I thought so.

Of course I missed my family and friends, so I took a short trip home to visit them, but when I returned to Guatemala, my ex was a different person. I'm not exaggerating. It was as if he had fallen out of love with me overnight. He was cold, moody and secretive. And he always seemed to be 'working'.

When I questioned him about the sudden changes, he got angry and abusive. The insults and lies got worse over time. Frankly, until then I had never heard some of the insults he levelled at me. I put up with it because I wanted so badly for the relationship to work and I was hoping that he would change back to the man I fell in love with. I tried everything I could to save the relationship, but nothing I did seemed to please him. I was confused and scared because I knew in my heart that it was the beginning of the end.

Eventually, I found out that he had met someone else while I was away and had been cheating on me with her since then. So I packed my bags and came back to Australia. It was a very tough decision, but I knew that I deserved better than to be treated with lies, insults and total disrespect.

I had lived in Sydney for most of my adult life, but I decided to move to sunny Brisbane for a fresh new start. It was not the smartest decision in hindsight. Put yourself in my shoes: I was heartbroken, jobless *and* now without family and friends in a strange city. I hit rock bottom.

However, being a stubborn, headstrong Taurus, I wasn't going to give up without a fight. Instead, I pulled out all the stops to get back on my feet again.

At first, of course, I had no idea where to start. I was lost. The breakup took so much out of me and my self-confidence plummeted; I doubted everything, from my own value as a woman to my ability to think and make decisions. I lost all my trust in people, especially men. Also, I thought that I had screwed up and now I was broken. So instead of finding love and passion again with an amazing man, going forward I could only settle for a lukewarm relationship with a 'nice' guy.

Luckily for me, I had some coaching a few years ago from a friend who was training to become a life coach, and it stuck with me. So I took a chance and decided to enrol in a coach training program. The program turned out to be a lifesaver. I learned a lot of powerful tools and strategies that allowed me to coach myself, challenge my unhelpful thoughts, release my painful emotions and ultimately heal my wounds. Instead of wallowing in those emotions and being stuck in old beliefs and patterns, I made a surprisingly quick recovery.

I discovered that I could adapt the tools and strategies to help other women who were going through difficult transitions in their lives. So after I finished the training, I started coaching private clients to help them make successful transitions, whether it was in the area of work, relationships or health. And that was my long answer to why I've written this book and why I'm passionate about helping women like you bounce back from breakups and heartaches.

Today I am convinced that, at least once in our lifetime, we will meet someone who completely changes the trajectory of our life, for better or for worse. And my ex was such a person. But of course I didn't know it back then. I was just following my heart. And my heart wanted what it wanted – him. I'm thankful, though, for all that I went through. I wouldn't be the person I am today without that part of my journey.

And I really like the person I am today.

How to Use This Book

Adversity is like a strong wind… It also tears away from us all but the things that cannot be torn, so that afterward we see ourselves as we really are, and not merely as we might like to be.
  – Arthur Golden
  Memoirs of a Geisha

I encourage you to put what you learn from this book into practice as soon as possible. We are inundated by so much information, with new books, blogs and podcasts being published every day. Information alone, however, is not enough, as awareness is only the first step.

What's more, with the easy access to information these days, many people – myself included – consume or even hoard information without actually putting it into use. And we wonder why our lives haven't changed.

Indeed, **there's a huge gap between knowing and doing, and until you bridge that gap, you won't be able to see real changes.**

There is a reason why they say information is not transformation. This also applies to ideas or tools that may seem very basic to you at first. Just because they seem obvious or basic doesn't mean they have been fully integrated into your life. Remember, ideas are nothing without action.

On the other hand, even though I will be offering many ideas, tools and strategies in each chapter of the book, don't try to implement more than a couple of things at once. Go with your gut and see what grabs your attention first. Stay focused and just start with one thing. Give it a go and see what happens. If it works, great. Keep it. If it doesn't, toss it aside.

Small baby-step changes aren't as sexy as big, overnight transformations, but they add up over time to larger and long-lasting transformations.

In other words, adopt an *experimental* mindset for your life. See your life as a big experiment. **When you reframe your life in this way, there are no setbacks or failures – only experiments and feedback.** From there you are free to make as many 'mistakes' as possible in your experiments, as long as you learn something every time.

Also, expect messiness, as there will be obstacles along the way. It's not easy because some of us have never started a new life with purpose before. We've followed a path given to us by our parents, peers and society at large. Alternatively, we may have lost our way after years of unhappy relationships and other life circumstances.

Therefore, it's a process of *unlearning* as much as learning, of subtracting and getting rid of our fears, false beliefs and negative patterns as well as adding new concepts and tools to your toolbox. Take your time and be patient with yourself. The healing process will not be linear. Instead, it will often feel like you are taking two steps forward and one step back!

Despite the ups and downs of your healing process, have faith that you are still on an overall upward trend. The trick is to keep the motivation and spirit up while working on yourself, and not to give up or give in to negative emotions and temptations.

That means while you are making your way through this book, be aware of unhealthy coping strategies. We will cover the common breakup mistakes in **chapter one**, so you can avoid them and stay on course with your healing journey.

1. The Day After

Rock bottom became the solid foundation on which I rebuilt my life.
   – J.K.Rowling

Top Breakup Mistakes

Here is a list of the top breakup mistakes that most people commit. By working through the book, I hope you will be able to avoid them, or at least notice it when you've committed them, so you can make a different choice.

1. You don't grieve; instead you numb yourself (Chapters 2 and 3)

When we are going through a breakup, we are in fact going through a grieving process. However, instead of letting yourself be with your emotions – yes, I mean all the hurt, confusion, anger, disappointment, longing, shame and guilt associated with the loss of a partner and the relationship itself – you avoid or even deny them. Instead of feeling them and then letting them go, you look for something or someone outside to distract or numb yourself so you don't have to feel those feelings.

We all have our vices – the thing (or two) we do to make ourselves feel better for now. Maybe it's TV, food or alcohol. Increasingly, it's social media. The list goes on. They are normal responses to stress but should only be indulged in moderation. While they may provide some short-term pain relief, they are also distractions that prevent you from focusing on yourself and on healing the root causes of your pain.

2. You keep in contact with your ex or stalk them on social media (Chapters 3 and 8)

By keeping in touch with your ex, you are holding on to your relationship beyond its expiry date. It's human nature to want to hold on to things and people we love, but there is a time to let go. By holding on to the ghost of your past relationship, you are not giving yourself the space to reconnect with yourself and heal from the breakup. You are also likely to get triggered every time you communicate with your ex and you lose focus on yourself and your own journey. Worse still, you might be lying to yourself and harbouring a secret wish for something more.

Even if you have officially cut off ties with your ex, you might end up stalking them on social media, participating in a comparison game instead of protecting yourself. Social media and other distractions suck up your time and energy that could be better spent on yourself. More often than not, you end up getting hurt when you see pictures of them having a great time or even starting a new relationship with other people. Why torture yourself? It's time to let go of your ex and close your 'ex file'.

3. You rebound immediately or you decide not to trust men... ever again (Chapters 6, 7 and 12)

Instead of holding on to your ex, you might get into a new relationship right away to fill the void they have left behind, or to give a quick boost to your self-esteem and feel desired again. Just like drugs and alcohol, relationships can be a powerful addiction, although they are not often viewed that way in our culture. Rather than grieving your loss, you find it easier to move on to a new relationship so you don't have to deal with your pain for now.

However, unless you have fully healed and rebuilt your self-worth, dating so early on after a breakup can be brutal. Also, you need a chance to figure out how to live your life without your ex and to get to know yourself again. It's hard to do that if you are already preoccupied with someone new.

On the other extreme, you over-learn your lessons from your heartbreak and think all men are bastards. You decide you don't want to be hurt like that ever again. You harden and build walls around your heart, choosing to stay single indefinitely and keeping any potential candidates at arm's length. Even if you find yourself dating or in a relationship, you have a hard time trusting your partner and are always on the lookout for red flags and anything negative.

4. You blame yourself or your ex endlessly (Chapters 5, 6 and 8)

Regardless of who initiated the breakup, breakups are painful and confusing. Sometimes you could see it coming, other times you are completely oblivious until it hits you like a bus. So you go looking for answers – or 'closure' – either from yourself and your ex, hoping to make sense of the mess you find yourself in and discharge some of the hurt that you feel.

It's very natural, or helpful even, to go through a period of intense self-reflection to assess the breakup and the parts you and your partner played in it. However, the trouble starts when you become obsessed and you can't stop ruminating about all the things you or your ex should have said or done differently, all the times they have hurt you (or vice versa), and indulging in negative talk – out loud or in your head – about yourself or your ex. Blaming makes you feel like a powerless victim and keeps you stuck in a continuous drama. This process can go on for weeks, months or even *years*.

5. You isolated yourself from your support network (Chapters 5 and 7)

It's quite common to want to spend time on your own when you are freshly out of a relationship. In fact, it can be really helpful for your healing process. The problem begins when you continue to withdraw and stay isolated for too long from your support network, wallowing in your sorrows, or feeling embarrassed over your 'failed' relationship and worrying that others will judge you. As a result, you don't keep up with family and friends, then you think nobody cares about you. It's a vicious cycle.

As for those who of you who are used to being very independent, you might think showing vulnerability is a sign of weakness or you find it incredibly hard to open up and be vulnerable, so you stay away from your support network and try to rebuild your life on your own.

6. You give up and you settle (Chapters 10–12)

As a result of your breakup, you now think, *What's the point? I'm broken and I'll never love or be loved again.* You feel like you've lost your sense of self and your direction in life now that you are no longer a wife or girlfriend. So you start drifting. You don't look after yourself like you used to, and you give up on the things you used to enjoy. You stop planning for your future and have nothing to look forward to. You feel like you are living the same day over and over again and all the joys have been drained out of your life.

When it comes to dating, you think it's easier to settle so at least you don't have to feel lonely again. You find yourself with 'nice guys' to whom you feel very little attraction, but you remind yourself that this is what real life is about: *No more dreaming, no more fun and joy. Just surviving and going through the motions.*

Grief

You have lost someone fundamental to your world. Give yourself permission to grieve your loss and to feel *all* the emotions you are experiencing. They are not abnormal and you haven't 'lost it'.

Indeed, divorce is said to be the second most stressful life event after the death of a loved one. Also, research has found that the rejection from a breakup can affect the body like cocaine withdrawal. So, don't beat yourself up for feeling the way you feel.

However, most people have a timeline of when they think they should be 'over' something. Forget your timeline. It's not a race, and you have nothing to prove to anyone, including to your ex or yourself. Give yourself the time to properly grieve the loss of your relationship.

According to Elisabeth Kübler-Ross, a famous psychiatrist and a pioneer in near-death studies, there are five stages of grief: shock and denial, anger, bargaining, depression and acceptance.

In a nutshell, here is how the grief cycle works: as you try to protect yourself from the immediate fallout from a breakup or divorce, shock and denial are a common first response to grief. Then anger sets in when you can no longer buffer your pain and are indignant at the unfairness of it all. You want to strike back and make your ex hurt as much as you do. This is followed by bargaining or magical thinking when you try to change the situation. Then when reality hits and you realise that you can't change it, sadness and depression set in. Finally, after some time you accept things as they are, make peace with it and are able to move on to the next chapter of your life.

Well, at least that's what it looks like in theory. Things are a lot messier in real life. You may stay in one of the stages for a long time, repeat a few stages, or skip a stage altogether. The model offers a general view, but each of us grieves in our own way and at our own pace. What I've learned is that you can't hurry the grieving process.

What you can do instead is to build conditions inside and around yourself that are conducive to acceptance, and welcome it when it comes.

Think about your current situation through the lens of the grief cycle and locate which stage you are at. Whatever stage you are at is fine, and know that it's normal and natural to feel whatever you are feeling.

For now, just know that you are going to weather some storms, but it won't last forever. It sounds trite, but there is light at the end of the tunnel and you will get through this. Along the journey, you'll learn that you can rely on yourself and there are wonderful things waiting for you on the other side, even though it may sound far-fetched to you now.

> I was lost in the immediate aftermath of my breakup. Even though I did all the 'right' things – I went to bed early, ate healthy food, exercised and stayed away from alcohol and other temptations – nothing I did came close to making me feel better. After a while it dawned on me that maybe I wasn't meant to feel better straight away. I was meant to grieve the loss of my relationship and to feel every single emotion of pain and despair.
>
> Realising this did make things easier in some ways. While my emotions changed like the weather outside and on my bad days I thought I was going out of my mind, at the same time I knew it was normal to feel the way I felt.
>
> For me, the moment finally came when I realised that I would never get the closure I wanted from him, and it was up to me to move on, with or without closure. Also, even though I was doing all the 'right' things to take care of myself physically, I needed to go inward to look at the deepest fears and old beliefs I'd held. I needed to step up and really give it my everything. So I did.

Three Healing Phases

Typically, we go through three healing phases after a breakup.

It's important to experience each phase of the healing process rather than trying to rush it. A breakup can be devastating, and we should take our time and treat ourselves with lots of tenderness and self-love, and not dismiss it out of hand.

Phase One – 'Tears': Shock and denial, pain and anger, bargaining, lashing out or withdrawal (3–6 months minimum)

This is the phase when your emotions are raw, messy and stormy. You can't avoid the emotional rollercoaster ride because it's a normal and natural part of the grief process, and *it's a reminder that you have really loved.* However, there are ways that you can help yourself go through this phase more quickly instead of just waiting for time to 'heal it all'. As mentioned before, time is a healer but not the only one, and it's too passive to depend only on it.

It's important to note that **we belong to a culture that doesn't value our emotional wounds as much as our physical ones.**

Imagine if you had a broken arm; would you try to ignore or even deny it? No, you would give yourself all the time, attention and care you need to heal from it. However, what we would often do with a broken heart is to rush through our healing or ignore it altogether.

Before I continue, let me share a quick word about emotions. While the intensity of your raw emotions will gradually reduce over time, just because things will get better doesn't mean it won't hurt right now. So accept your feelings and know that things will *suck* for a while, especially if you are at the early stage of your breakup.

For now, the most important thing is to **shift your focus from your ex back to yourself so you can start your healing journey** during this phase. I understand that it's a lot easier said than done. Love can be a powerful drug, and to try to force yourself to not think about your ex is like trying not to think about a pink elephant. (You are thinking about it now, aren't you?)

Therefore, I don't suggest that you suppress your thoughts and feelings. Many studies have shown that thought suppression doesn't work anyway and would actually make things worse. Rather, I'm advocating changing your focus so you can naturally untangle yourself from your ex over time. Whatever you focus on grows, and, conversely, whatever you don't withers away. This book will offer some tips to help you do just that in **chapter three**.

Phase Two – 'Clearing': Inner work and reflection, isolation and loneliness, depression, beginning of re-entry (6–18 months)

Congratulations, you've made it through the first phase! You are now over the worst of your pain, and trying to make an effort to re-engage with the world. You are no longer riding an emotional rollercoaster and are starting to see things more clearly, even just marginally.

However, you probably have been spending quite a lot of time on your own to process your hot emotions. Or you may have deliberately hidden from others because you are embarrassed of your 'failed' relationship and worried about others' judgment. It's okay to be on our own, but don't stay there for too long, especially if you find yourself feeling isolated or even depressed. Call in your support network, or start building one if you have distanced your friends due to your breakup.

This is where I come in mostly with my private coaching work, helping my clients build the bridge between phase one and phase three. However, this is also the stage where a lot of people want to rush through or ignore altogether. They want to get to the 'other side'. But just as you can't hurry the healing of a broken arm, you also can't do it with a broken heart.

Instead, use this in-between time well. Since you are already outside your comfort zone, you might as well make the best of this time to work on yourself: to rediscover your authentic self and let go of the negative and welcome the positive, rebuild your confidence and self-worth to love and trust yourself, close your ex file once and for all and set healthy boundaries, and take care of your body and mind like it's nobody's business. Don't be in a hurry to get back inside your comfort zone, where it's, well, comfortable. However, there is not much room for learning and growth.

Phase Three – 'Peace': Acceptance, meaning, upturn, re-invention, reconnection, fun and play (after 12–18 months)

By this phase, you will have processed your pain, accepted your breakup as final and irreversible, and started to let go of and make peace with your past. You will have learnt the lessons from it and even found some hidden blessings.

Moreover, by working on yourself in phase two, you will have regained your sense of control and trust in yourself and others, rebuilt a new sense of self and found a new purpose in life, and will be taking daily actions towards your goals and dreams.

You will also have a more loving relationship with yourself, or at least will have assumed personal responsibility and have stopped blaming yourself or others for your breakup. Fun and play will have returned to your life and you will be now experiencing more ease and freedom. Even peace.

Finally, you will be now ready to go out into the world either as a single person or in another relationship and need support on how to do that. By the way, if you are looking for a new relationship and you did your inner work properly in phase two, you will be able to attract a different calibre of men who are not afraid of strong, confident women.

(In this book, we will cover all three phases, but an emphasis has been placed on phase two, as it is the critical phase in which you can work through a lot of issues to reach the final phase of acceptance.)

Conscious Breakup

But you can't get to any of these truths by sitting in a field smiling beatifically, avoiding your anger and damage and grief. Your anger and damage and grief are the way to the truth. We don't have much truth to express unless we have gone into those rooms and closets and woods and abysses that we were told not to go in to.
– Anne Lamott
Bird by Bird

I believe that a breakup is a doorway to personal development and fulfilment, if you let it be – consciously, courageously and lovingly. There is immense growth for you mentally, emotionally and spiritually. Indeed, **heartbreaks are one of the best ways because they bring up so much stuff that you get the chance to finally clean them up and really heal once and for all.**

Some examples of the 'stuff' that may surface in the aftermath of a breakup include your fears – fears of being alone or abandoned, of being not good enough, as well as your longing for love and attention outside of yourself, your pattern of placing the source of your happiness in another person, and attracting the same unavailable or uncommitted men over and over again.

However, many of us – myself included until my last breakup – see breakups as a mistake or failure. We run away from it or put it into the too hard basket and 'move on' as soon as possible, whatever that may look like to you. We look for something or someone external to distract ourselves so we don't have to deal with all our 'stuff'. Typically, we resort to one or more of these three kneejerk reactions:

- We may go straight back into a relationship – either with our ex or someone new;

- We throw ourselves into our work, parenting or something else to fill the void;

- We shut down and do nothing, giving up on love entirely or believing that time will heal our wounds.

However, until you have really resolved your hurt feelings and old beliefs (aka your 'baggage') as well as your negative thinking patterns, which will generate more baggage in the future, **you are destined to repeat the same patterns and the same relationship dance, just with different people down the road.** At the same time, you run the risk of getting in a downward spiral and becoming jaded.

Indeed, we know how to start and end a relationship, but we don't know how to *complete* one. By learning how to properly complete a relationship, we can turn a breakup into a breakthrough and use it as an opportunity to re-design an exciting future the way we want.

Shifting the Definition

More deeply, in addition to inviting you to see breakups as a catalyst to personal growth and fulfilment, I'd like you to re-examine the old meaning we give to the breakdown of a relationship or marriage in our culture. A breakup means something has gone wrong. It has failed, and, by extension, so have the two people involved in the relationship. It's such a deep-seated belief that we rarely question it.

However, I encourage you to consider the alternative. Not all relationships are meant to last a lifetime, and it's perfectly okay. While a long and happy union is something to which we can aspire, it doesn't have to be the only standard by which to measure relationship 'success'. There are legitimate reasons for a relationship to end, and trying to keep a dead relationship going doesn't serve anyone.

If we shift our focus away from only the negative impacts of a breakup, a union of any duration – from a few months to fifty years – offers many gifts for both parties, especially if we use the experience to learn and grow as a person. Viewed from this perspective, the outcome may be different but the relationship is no less successful than a life-long union.

For example, often we associate breakups or divorces with a host of negative feelings and states: pain, fear, anxiety, loneliness, low self-esteem, loss of identity and purpose, conflicts, parenting challenges, financial difficulties, instability and uncertainty.

While some or even all of these may be true for you at certain stages of your healing journey, let's look at some new definitions that may also be just as true. For example: relief, excitement, possibility, independence, new love, new friends, an opportunity to rebuild your life the way you want, valuable life lessons and self-discovery, confidence, healing, peace and freedom.

These new definitions, and therefore new ways of looking at a breakup, will change the way you cope with it. While they might seem like a fairytale at this early stage, with the healing work we are about to embark on, you will begin to shift your perspective and feel excited about your future.

2. Riding the Emotional Storm with Ease

Pain

It's completely normal to feel like you've been hit by a truck and every cell in your body hurts like hell. Even if you were the one who decided to end the relationship, the reality of a breakup or divorce would still shake your world. It's also completely normal to feel all over the place now, at times strong and self-sufficient while at other times hopeless and helpless.

Unfortunately, there is no magic wand to take away all of your pain. But there are ways you can lessen it. For now, it's important to remember that things will get better, even though you can't see it now. The cloud will lift a little as everyday passes *and* as you do the work. So focus on getting through today, or even just this hour or this minute. As Scarlett O'Hara says in *Gone with the Wind*, 'tomorrow is another day'.

To feel pain is to be human. That said, when our heart breaks, the pain is so intense that we often don't want to experience it. So we avoid, suppress or even deny it. We put up every barrier to resist pain. Being with it seems unbearable.

It doesn't help either that we live in a world that fears pain and tells us to deny our heartbreak. We are so conditioned to try to fix everything that we forget we are humans after all, that it's normal and healthy to feel pain.

Let Yourself Feel

As you will discover, **while it *feels* easier to bury pain now, not facing it will bring you more pain in the long run**. The only way out of pain is *through* it.

The more you ignore or suppress how you feel, the harder it will be to let go and move through it. Resisting the pain takes enormous energy and when you finally surrender to feeling the pain, there is a sense of relief and freedom. So sit in the 'fire' and let it transform you.

On the other hand, if you don't let yourself feel, you will harden and become increasingly closed and contracted. There will be no true healing, and these feelings will come back up to bite you.

In fact, research has shown that while engaging with negative emotions – disappointment, anger, shame, etc – may initially increase our experience of these emotions, approaching such emotions in a non-judgmental and self-loving way will diffuse them relatively quickly.

Even though it's healthy to feel your pain, it's important not to exaggerate it. Things are bad as they are, for now at least, so focus on the facts, not on the worst case scenarios.

Better still, try look for the silver linings. For example, if you have been in an unhealthy relationship, perhaps there is a part of you that feels relieved. Or even a little excited about the future without your controlling, abusive ex.

True Healing

True healing, despite what you've heard, is not as smooth as you think.

First, it's messy, and it's not going to look like a straight line. Instead, you are going to have some good days, some bad days, and some very bad days when you don't even want to get out of bed and you feel like you've lost the will to live. Expect that, and remind yourself that *this is just for now*, or *this, too, shall pass*.

Your mind will play tricks on you when you are down and out, so don't react to all the self-flagellations and worst-case scenarios that your mind conjures up during those times. Delay making any major decisions or taking any hasty actions. Go inward and heal.

Second, you may be able to speed up your healing process to a certain extent by supporting yourself with the strategies and tools from this book and surrounding yourself with supportive people. However, at the end of the day, it's still a *process*. So it will take time, probably longer than you think it 'should'. Drop the expectations and just do your best. Don't think you 'should' be further ahead than you are at any stage of your healing process; accept where you are with kindness and grace.

As a coach, I love working with people in pain. (No, I'm not a sadist – quite the contrary.) I'm a sensitive introvert so it hurts me to see others in pain. However, I'm also deeply aware that many of us are so used to feeling uncomfortable or even crappy, stuck in a dead-end relationship, job or life. We can stay stuck there for years, if not decades.

On the other hand, when we are in pain, like when we face a breakup or divorce, it grabs all our attention, snaps us out of our daily routines and forces us to stop and ask some serious questions: *What did I do wrong?*, *How did I get here?* and *Who am I?* In other words, **pain is a way into your tender underbelly where your fears and wounds reside; it breaks you wide open so that the light can get in through the cracks**, and you'll finally see your life as it really is.

15

Let's face it, inner work is hard, and nobody wants to do it unless we are forced to. When we are feeling stuck, we are in survival mode and all we want is to get through the day and we don't have the energy to do the deep discovery work. However, when pain forces us to stop in our tracks, we have the choice to clear out all the old beliefs and patterns that no longer serve us, make up our own rules that do, and finally go after our deepest desires and dreams. We become the creator of our future.

I'm guilty of resisting pain all through my life. My proactive, pragmatic side wants to ignore my feelings and go straight to doing and fixing – in order to avoid the pain and to try to control the situation. The last thing I want is to feel like a helpless victim.

In my youth, that translated to sweeping things under the carpet and moving on as soon as possible. I didn't take the time to look within and really heal after each breakup; rather, I looked outside for solutions. Luckily for me, 'moving on' for me for most parts didn't involve jumping into another relationship; it involved me taking back my time and rediscovering my interests. And I had many of them, thankfully.

So, in between my relationships, I travelled a lot. I exercised more. I read all the books and binge-watched all the movies and TV shows that I didn't get a chance to read and watch while I was busy losing myself in the relationship. I did countless courses and workshops. I even made efforts to reconnect with my old friends and to go out and meet new people.

But on the whole, I was on my own a lot. The loneliness from my self-imposed isolation was intense but I brushed it aside, just as I brushed aside the hurt and pain of my breakups.

Looking back, things could have been worse. I chose relatively harmless distractions instead of trying to fill the void with self-destructive activities or substances such as drugs and alcohol. However, they were distractions nonetheless; I was still seeking temporary fixes outside.

Instead of keeping myself busy, I wish I had known the power of self-compassion and self-reflection and spent more time just being with myself and my emotions, as well as being open and vulnerable with my family and friends and asking for their support.

Perhaps I didn't have enough courage and strength back then. Now that I am older and, supposedly, wiser, I know courage is a practice, not just a feeling. We practise small acts of courage every day. That means feeling *all* our emotions rather than fixing or denying them, and asking or support to lessen our burden and speed up our process of healing.

Emotions, Emotions, Emotions

It would be impossible to estimate how much time and energy we invest in trying to fix, change and deny our emotions – especially the ones that shake us at our very core, like hurt, jealousy, loneliness, shame, rage and grief.
– Debbie Ford

I feel that there are a lot of misunderstandings around emotions. So let's clear up a few things before moving on to cultivating more awareness and ease around our emotions.

First, it's important to remind yourself that every emotion serves a **purpose**. In other words, there are no 'good' or 'bad' feelings per se, even though we like to label them as such.

Take anger as an example; we often label it as 'bad' and try to deny or suppress it. However, anger usually arises when we feel a sense of injustice, like when we've been treated unfairly or disrespectfully by our ex or an insensitive friend. It's a very powerful emotion and energises us – at least in the short term – so we get into action to try to change the situation. Therefore, anger is a necessary and useful emotion in some situations.

However, too much of anything isn't good. Drowning in *unnecessary* negative emotions can be just as harmful as bottling them up. We may end up lashing out at our ex and then feel ashamed of our words or actions the next day. So there needs to be a **balance**. It's healthy to feel your feelings, but there's a difference between feeling your feelings and wallowing in them.

The way we wallow in or perpetuate our feelings is to ruminate and continuously return to the 'scene of the crime'. Since whatever we focus on grows, we allow these feelings to grow disproportionately and eventually occupy our whole mind, accumulating them instead of just letting them flow through us like what emotions are meant to do.

Also, since we think certain feelings are 'bad' and therefore we shouldn't feel them, we usually add another layer of **judgment** on top of our feelings. This is what the Buddhists call 'the second arrow'. Buddhists make a clear distinction between *pain*, which is an inevitable part of life, and *suffering*, which is pain plus all the judgments and stories we add on top of it.

For example, we had a fight with our ex-partner, and we tell ourselves that we shouldn't have 'lost it' and that we were too intense or too angry, feeling even more miserable as a result and maybe take it out on the kids or the dog – instead of simply letting it go, making up or apologising if we were in the wrong.

Whether you subscribe to the self-inflicted nature of suffering, in any case, with so much of our attention and time going into our heads, ruminating and judging, it's easy to see why our feelings can become all-consuming.

Last but not least, we all have our favourite **go-to emotion** (or emotions) which we evoke automatically. For some people it's anger, for others it's anxiety or sadness. These emotions get triggered as if we were on autopilot, and it takes awareness and a lot of practice to bring our state of mind back to a balanced state, or equanimity.

Emotional Intelligence

The most important question is not how to get rid of our own wounds, but how to make our wounds a source of healing.
– Henri Nouwen
The Wounded Healer

We all want to feel better. I'm not just talking about how to feel 'better' emotions such as joy and confidence, but to get better at feeling all of our emotions – the good, the bad and the ugly.

Indeed, when we learn how to *feel* better, we feel *better*. Not only that, we would be so much less afraid! Instead of wasting our energy on resisting our negative emotions, we would be *invincible*. **Imagine how powerful you would feel if there were no emotions you were afraid to feel.**

However, feeling better isn't as simple as it sounds. We have to feel our whole range of emotions, rather than resist some of them while welcoming others. That means we also have to notice negative thinking and automatic reactions. The aim is to build trust in yourself that you can handle *all* emotions, so you don't have to protect yourself from *any* emotions. You have to put in the work constantly to feel good. But it's so worth it.

There are two aspects to this: having a healthy attitude towards your emotions in general, and managing them in the moment.

1. There are no 'bad' emotions

Feeling our emotions – especially the negative ones – is the price we pay for living a *wholehearted* life, and in the case of breakups, it's essential for our healing. However, it's uncomfortable and we are often tempted to avoid, suppress or numb our difficult emotions.

But according to author and researcher Brené Brown, "you cannot selectively numb emotion. When we numb [hard feelings], we numb joy, we numb gratitude, we numb happiness." In other words, when we numb our lows, we also numb our highs.

Not only that, we become disconnected from the wisdom and truth that our feelings point to. As mentioned earlier, every emotion serves a purpose. So not only are all our feelings necessary, but the ones we have deemed unworthy are particularly enlightening. They point us to the parts of us that have been hidden or repressed, and guide us to true healing and to loving every aspect of ourselves.

It is through allowing *all* our feelings that we really get to know ourselves and truly bounce back better than ever.

2. Don't wallow

On the other hand – and we have already touched on this earlier – there is a difference between feeling your feelings and wallowing in them. Whatever you focus on grows. Therefore, it's about finding that balance between *being* with your pain and other negative emotions, while at the same time not dwelling on them endlessly.

At the end of the day, emotions are energies that need to be felt, expressed and then discharged, otherwise they get trapped inside of you and accumulate over time. So, go ahead and find healthy ways to feel and express your feelings. Just don't obsess about them.

3. More importantly, don't act out in unhealthy behaviour

We often resort to doing or fixing so as not to feel our emotions. There is a place for distractions, especially in the moment when the emotions can be overwhelming and we are trying to buffer ourselves from the avalanche. However, make sure the distractions do not hurt you or become addictive crutches for you.

In the long term, we are aiming to soften the hold that emotions have on us and to open up the *space* between how we feel and what we do, so we can choose appropriate actions independent of how we feel. *We become in charge of our feelings, not the other way around.*

4. You are not your emotions

One thing I find really helpful is to know that your feelings are fleeting and not to over-identify with them. Remind yourself that you have your feelings, but you are *not* your feelings. A good way to do this is to change your pronoun from 'I' to 'you'. According to research, when we use 'you' to make sense of our experiences, it allows us to look at them from a distance and normalise them.

For example, when we are in a bad emotional place, we can say to ourselves, *what doesn't kill you makes you stronger*. This ability to move beyond ourselves to see the shared, universal experiences enables us to derive broader meanings from personal events. In other words, we are able to see the big picture, instead of being sucked in by our emotions and our stories.

5. Experience – don't rationalise – your emotions regularly

Lastly, for those of us who are logical by nature (or due to our upbringing or education), we like to rationalise away our feelings rather than feeling them. We think about our emotions and believe that we can manage or even get rid of our negative emotions with our thoughts. After all, we have been taught that we have to 'think things through'.

However, it's hard – if not downright impossible – to rationalise emotions. We are rational as well as emotional beings, and our problems have both rational and emotional components. Hence, it's better to take an integrated approach, rather than seeing them as totally separate and opposite in nature.

Emotions are also less overwhelming if you are open to experiencing them on a regular basis. Do this often while you are in your normal states and when your tank is full. So when something major happens like a breakup or a serious illness, you are more prepared to experience the tsunami of emotions, instead of feeling overwhelmed by your emotions that you *feel like* you have no choice but to either explode (fight) or run away from them (flight).

What to Do in the Moment

So what can you do in the moment of experiencing a negative emotion, or a cascade of negative emotions?

First, **breathe!** Often we forget to breathe when we are under stress. Experiencing a negative emotion can be stressful, and there is no easier way to release the tension in the moment than by breathing.

In fact, breathing activates our parasympathetic nervous system, which is in charge of relaxation and of lowering our fight-and-flight stress response. So pause and take a deep breath (or two or three), until you start to calm down.

Secondly, and this might sound a bit controversial, but I'm an advocate of having **a big, messy cry**, *especially* if that's something you don't normally give yourself permission to do. Yelling or screaming is also encouraged.

Now let me elaborate on this point a bit more. Some of us are hesitant to cry, yell or scream when we are upset. I understand completely. It took me years to learn to cry, at least in public.

> I had a scalding accident when I was 11 or 12 years old. I ended up with second-degree burns on my hands and forearms, so my parents rushed me to the hospital. We were all sitting in the emergency room and I was bawling my eyes out. Then I remember, to this day, how my dad looked at me straight in the eye and told me to shut up. I was so stunned that I stopped crying right away. And, at that moment, I decided to never cry again, at least in public.
>
> My shock was partly due to the fact that I had always been my dad's little princess. Don't get me wrong, he had a

quick temper and I wouldn't have wanted to upset him, but somehow I managed to get away with a lot of things as a child.

For the next twenty-one years until my dad's passing when I was 33, I cried very, very rarely. It was like a once-a-year event for me. And I certainly didn't cry at all in public.

It wasn't that I didn't get sad. I did, but I basically had shut down and lost the ability to cry. At one stage I even thought perhaps my tear glands were faulty!

In the meantime, as my dad got older, he 'mellowed out' and we grew even closer. So when my dad passed away, it opened a floodgate. I spent the whole year after his death crying. I cried in my room. I cried when I talked to my friends about him. I cried when I was driving (which, by the way, was a health hazard because I could barely see the road…). I cried whenever something reminded me of him. I cried everywhere. I was an inconsolable, sobbing mess, but I was grieving a loss so great that that I didn't care what other people thought.

On the other hand, even though a large part of me was sad, a small part of me was relieved – I felt like I finally had the permission to be myself again. The real me was a lot more 'girly' and softer than what he had wanted me to be. It was the part of me who would cry when she was upset, rather than stuffing it down and putting on a brave face.

While crying, yelling or screaming won't resolve the actual problem, it will discharge some of the pent-up energies inside of you and make you feel better, calmer and clearer in the moment, so why not? You can cry, yell or scream to your heart's content in private.

On the other hand, if you choose to do it in public or to someone else, and if you think you've overstepped the line and hurt their feelings in doing so, you can always go back and apologise to them afterwards.

If, however, you find yourself unable to cry for whatever reason, you can try **positive distractions**, in particular those that take you out of your head – where you've been spending way too much time anyway if you're having prolonged, intense feelings – and into your body, so get your butt moving.

Whether it's working out, going for a yoga class or just taking a long walk, these distractions will buy you some time to calm down, so you can deal with your emotions more appropriately afterwards. What's more, as emotions are packets of energy, it's good to find a way to physically discharge them. When you move your body, you shift your energy.

Lastly, **writing** is another helpful tool. While it may seem like the last thing you want to do when you are going through an emotional storm, it's just another way to get out of your head. Often we feel overwhelmed because we carry so much stuff in our head, so writing is a great way is to create mental space by dumping everything in your head onto paper or a computer.

Writing also helps you to clarify your thoughts, and things always seem more manageable when you have them in front of you instead of letting them go around in circles in your head. It will help you to describe, make sense of and process your feelings. There is magic in writing things down, so try it!

3. Inside Job

When we are no longer able to change a situation, we are challenged to change ourselves.
    – Viktor Frankl

Now What?

As women, we often define ourselves by our roles: we are a wife or girlfriend, a mum, a daughter, a sister, and so on. Unfortuntately, we also tend to get lost in our intimate relationships, so we merge with our partner and our sense of self becomes very blurred.

When our relationship breaks down, we lose our 'label' and subsequently our individual identity. Not to mention we have also lost our identity as a couple and all our shared dreams and hopes for the future.

If we are no longer a wife or girlfriend, who are we?

We find ourselves in this uncomfortable, scary in-between space – limbo land – where we are no longer our old self but our new self is not yet formed.

With the loss of identity and shared future comes the loss of purpose. We don't know where we belong and what we are supposed to do anymore, and it can feel confusing and scary and totally out of control. "Now what?" is a common question I hear a lot from my clients at this stage of their journey.

So after you have dealt with your raw emotions, it's time to start reclaiming yourself. Better still, you may want to create a brand new you. It's not going to happen overnight but you will get more clarity as you go on your inner journey.

For now, let's look at a common occurrence in the aftermath of a breakup: our tendency to look for a quick fix. It's understandable to feel like our ex has left a huge void in our life, and we are tempted to try to fill it quickly with another relationship, work, new friends or interests.

Relationships, in particular, can be addictive. We all know someone – or it could even be at times ourselves – who jumps immediately from one relationship to another. That person never seems to take any time for herself between breakups to grieve, heal and remember who she *really* is. They use relationships as an excuse to never focus on themselves or on their personal growth.

The same can happen with work, new friends or interests, or other addictions such as drugs, alcohol and food, all of which are outside our control and offer only fleeting pleasures. They are cheap substitutes and don't give us a sense of lasting fulfilment that is independent of anyone or anything else.

The answer isn't out 'there'. We forget that it's an *inside job* all along. Everything starts from within.

Indeed, the lows of a breakup or divorce really show us the importance of getting to the heart of what makes us happy and fulfilled. The void left behind by your ex may be unbearable at first, but it also points you to what might have been missing in your life all along that you've covered up by being in a relationship. Now is the perfect time to be brave and take the steps to make those things happen in your life.

So, instead of using relationships, work or another quick fix as a crutch, use this time after your breakup wisely *and* bravely. Learn to shift your focus back to yourself, to go inward and reconnect with yourself and your true desires.

Because, even though your relationship with your ex had broken down, **you still have the most important relationship in your life – your relationship with yourself!**

This relationship doesn't get much love and attention because more often than not we take it for granted. (We will look at the details of how to love and care for yourself in **chapter six**.)

Your True Self

Once we realise that the answer isn't out there, we can start making our way back to ourselves. Our true self is who we are looking to reconnect at this stage of our healing.

So what, or who, is our true self? I believe that we are made up of different selves. (However, I'm not talking about having schizophrenia or a split personality!) Our true self – also known as our essence, inner wisdom or guide, higher self, Buddha nature, and so on – is the authentic part of ourselves that we have often ignored for a long time for fear of being not enough, different or unpopular.

Instead, we try to be someone else while letting our inner critic run our life. The good news is that our true self waits patiently to come out. One of the best ways to reconnect with our true self is through our intuition. Your intuition is how your true self speaks to you.

However, we often end up questioning ourselves and our intuition after a breakup because we feel it has let us down. The truth is, it hasn't let us down – if we are completely honest, we were the ones who had ignored our intuition and all the red flags.

And it's easy to ignore our intuition. Unlike our inner critic, which is loud and repetitive, our true self is often more quiet and subtle, and therefore can be easily drowned out with all the 'noise' inside and around us.

On top of that, our intuition is like a muscle – use it or risk losing it. So if you've ignored it long enough, you will have a hard time hearing or feeling it. Luckily, once you start listening to it regularly, the gates are open again. The best way to listen is to get quiet. By learning to listen to your true self through your intuition, this will go a long way towards rebuilding your trust in yourself and in others.

So back in 2012 when I fell head over heels in love with my ex, I abandoned everything to be with him; I listened to my heart but not my gut. I wasn't nervous when I made the travel arrangements, quit my job, got rid of my apartment, or even got on the flight.

But after I landed and was on my way in the bus to his city, I started to get nervous that he wouldn't show up at the bus stop at all! He did show up that day, but I think my gut was trying to tell me something all this time. I wished I had listened to it then.

No Contact Rule

The biggest secret to shifting your focus back to yourself and the quickest way to recover from your breakup is – drum roll, please – the No Contact rule (NC rule).

The rule itself is pretty straight forward: it involves not contacting your ex for three months minimum – and that means *all* forms of communication. In today's digitally connected world, this translates to a digital detox too.

In addition to not calling, texting or meeting your ex in person, you also want to unfriend them on Facebook or any other social media platforms and apps.

In fact, I would go a step further and hide mutual friends' or his family's newsfeeds, as well as deleting Facebook and other similar apps from your phone, so you are not tempted to check social media in a moment of loneliness or boredom.

All these actions will help you detach, shift your focus and thereby reduce your obsessive thoughts about your ex that comes with the territory – what happened, what you or they should have done differently, etc. Of course, your obsessive rumination may still continue, but in time it will happen less frequently and with less intensity. It's worth repeating that whatever you focus on grows, and conversely whatever you don't focus on withers away.

Consequently, you will most likely feel less distress and less desire for your ex. Sometimes you only need a couple of weeks to see a difference *if* you don't give in.

However, you may need to modify the NC rule a little if you have children and work with your ex. This means you have to keep your contacts and discussions limited to topics concerning your children or work.

Benefits

The NC rule will create the physical and emotional distance between you and your ex so you can start to *untangle*, rather than continue to see you and your ex as one fused entity. And, by untangling, it will help shift your focus back on yourself.

Not only can you shift your focus back to yourself, the bonus of the NC rule is that you also don't have to deal with all the bullshit your ex is up to: the abuse, stalking, jealousy and other negative emotions – any of which can seriously do your head in. Instead, you free yourself from their influences and move forward with your own brand new life.

And if you don't follow the NC rule? Well, nothing. *Nothing changes if nothing changes.*

You will continue to be stuck in an unhappy or even abusive relationship longer than you want to or is good for you. So the choice is yours – you can decide a new future for yourself by taking matters into your own hands; or you can continue to give away your power, and therefore your happiness, to your ex.

Remember, too, that the NC rule isn't permanent, so once you have reclaimed your separate identity from your ex, reduced your obsessive rumination and regained clarity about your situation, you can start communicating with your ex again in a way that is healthy and respectful.

Relapses

Be aware: just as you are surfacing, your ex may show up to pull you back under. Don't allow him or her to undo all your hard work.

Having no contact is difficult, so if you fall off the wagon, don't beat yourself up! It happens to everyone. But instead of quitting the NC rule altogether over one or two relapses, resolve to restart your NC rule again as soon as possible. Better still, put together a list of triggers and solutions ahead of time, so you are prepared to do the right thing when you are challenged.

In fact, as part of any change process, relapsing is an important part of the process where you fall back into your old pattern. As long as you don't throw in the towel, you will eventually find it easier to stay on the wagon. So be patient with yourself and aim for less contact over time.

I recommend cultivating a sense of *good-humoured patience*, where you don't take yourself, your setbacks and so-called 'failures' too seriously. You will expect to fail from time to time, and when you do, you will be prepared to jump back on the wagon and keep going instead of giving up.

Now over to you:
Do you want to give the No Contact rule a go? Why or why not? Be honest with your answers. It's ok that you don't want to give it a go now. You can always come back to this later.

> After I broke up with my ex and came back home, I kept receiving emails and calls from him. I couldn't help but answer them at first, but after a month or two I realised that it was doing my head in, and my desire for him was growing even stronger. I wanted to jump onto the next flight and go back to Central America to be with him!
>
> So I decided to stop cold turkey. At the end of the year, I wrote him a final 'goodbye' email and then set up my Gmail account to filter out his emails so they wouldn't appear in my inbox. I had no contact with him since then. It was really hard at first. But with the temptations gone, I was able to shift all my time and energy back on myself rather than trying to make him happy and to revive the relationship.

It was hard work, but I believe that it would have been even harder in the long term if I had stayed. The relationship had passed its expiry date.

Ending it, while extremely painful, was the right thing to do. He was never going to go back to the person he used to be, and I could have easily wasted a few more months or even years waiting for miracles to happen. I think my survival instincts to cut all ties saved me from going down the path of no return.

Other Strategies

What lies behind us and what lies before us are small matters compared to what lies within us. And when we bring what is within us out into the world, miracles happen.
   – Henry Stanley Haskins

Apart from the NC rule, there are other strategies that will help you focus on yourself to get clarity about your situation and to help you heal.

1. Honest self-reflection

Now that the worst of your emotional storm is over and you are not yet in another relationship, this is the perfect time to take a look at who you really are without these 'labels' and do the inner work you've been putting off. It will also make the rest of the healing journey easier.

Ask yourself the big questions: *Who am I?* and *What do I want?* Also, explore your values, passions, strengths, needs and wants.

A great tool for self-reflection is **journalling**. It allows you to look inward, offload and process your thoughts and emotions, and is therefore very cathartic. It's also a great way to track your progress over time to see how far you have come, including all the lessons and realisations you have had.

2. Be authentic

Be yourself, because everyone else is already taken! Don't be who you think you 'should' be in order to meet others' or your own expectations or rules. Now is the perfect time to break free from them! The self-reflection and journalling will help you become more self-aware, and you can start living your life more authentically based on your greater self-awareness.

However, in order to be authentic and live an authentic life, you need *courage*. It takes courage to stop trying to be anyone else and do or say anything because you think that's what's expected. It's not about 'fake it until you make it'. **It's not even about being your 'best self' as it is about being your real, whole self, with all your loveable – and not so loveable – parts.** Indeed, they say you can't have virtues without courage, so in a way, courage is a precursor to all virtues. (We will look more closely at it in **chapter four.**)

Also, I know this may sound far-fetched to those of you who don't even like and cannot find anything loveable in yourselves. If this sounds like you, learning to love and nurture yourself would be a game changer. Check out **chapter six** to learn more about how to be kinder to yourself and to become a person you love.

3. Nourish yourself

There's something to be said about having familiar routines when everything around you is changing or falling apart, so make sure you look after yourself. Go back to the basics – eating a healthy diet, moving your body even if it's just a walk in the park, and having plenty of rest. The mind-body connection means that when we are doing something physical, we can start to feel emotionally strong again.

Moreover, when we have a healthy and strong body, our mind is also stronger and less prone to negativity or depression. If you think you don't have time to exercise or prepare healthy meals, try getting sick! (We will cover more of this in **chapter six** in the section on self-care.)

4. Support yourself

Having great support in your life helps you to focus your attention on yourself. Instead of trying to do everything yourself, part of supporting yourself is to ask for the right support from others. You are not alone and there is help available – personal and professional – if you are willing to ask for it. This also includes finding accountability buddies, as having good intentions is not enough. (We'll go into more detail on this in **chapter seven.**)

Loneliness

*I wish I could show you when you are lonely or in darkness,
the astonishing light of your own being.*
   – Hafiz of Shiraz

In the process of shifting our focus away from our ex, we will often feel a void in our life left behind by them. That void creates a profound sense of loneliness, and it is one of the main reasons why some people keep breaking their No Contact rule.

Given the NC rule is the foundation to shifting your focus back to yourself and the quickest way to recover from your breakup in the initial days, here are some ways to ease your loneliness.

First, **know the difference between solitude and loneliness.**

Just because you are alone doesn't mean that you have to feel lonely, or that you will be lonely for the rest of your life. Learn to appreciate and enjoy solitude, which offers peace, calm, space and opportunity to connect with your deeper self. This is especially valuable after a breakup.

Second, **remember that you are not really alone.**

The person you have spent every minute of every day of your life with is you! I know it may be hard to digest at first – and it sounds super cheesy – but you are your own soulmate. So embrace that, appreciate yourself, and give yourself the love that you crave.

However, we are often told that we can only be happy when we are in a relationship. The truth is, we don't need to be in a relationship to be happy!

There are plenty of people who are single either by choice or by circumstances who are happier, or at least no less happy, than couples. The grass isn't greener over 'there'. It's human nature to want things that we don't have – so people in a relationship want the freedom and excitement that singles have, while singles want the security and stability that a relationship offers.

Third, it helps to **remind yourself that other people feel unworthy, awkward and lonely too.**

Even the most extroverted and sociable among us feel lonely from time to time. It's part of the human experience. So, just as we feel compassion for anyone else lonely and isolated, you also deserve this for yourself. Don't beat yourself up for feeling lonely and wanting to have a special someone in your life or be closer to those who are already in your life.

Finally, **learn to accept loneliness.**

By simply staying with the feeling of loneliness – or any other negative feelings for that matter – it will lessen its hold over you. If you can make peace with it, you will be reaching out to others because you want to, not because you need to. In other words, you do it out of desire, not fear or desperation.

If you are ready to reach out, below are some practical tips:

1. **Be proactive.** Fight the urge to isolate and put yourself out there. Don't wait for an invitation. Instead, take a risk and invite people to coffee, lunch or a movie. What's the worst that can happen? You'll just end up where you were before. On the other hand, they might say yes. People are a lot nicer than you think. Also, don't forget other people are afraid of rejections too, and perhaps they are just waiting for you to ask them!

2. **Open yourself up.** Allow yourself to be vulnerable in conversations and other interactions. You don't have to show only the best side of you. Experiment by sharing aspects of yourself, including your feelings, memories, dreams, quirks, etc. This will help you feel more seen and understood, and inspire others to open up too. The more you are able to share with one another, the most likely you will see that we are all in the same boat together.

3. **Ask for what you need.** Tell people what you need from them to ease your loneliness. Most people respond to direct, specific requests for support such as "I'd really like to go for coffee next weekend if you are free," rather than a general vague request like "Let's hang out sometime." Give it a try; you might be surprised! And, if they don't, at least you will find out sooner than later. Remember to follow up too; we are all busy these days and it's easy to let things slip from our mind.

4. **Be patient.** Forming and keeping relationships takes time and effort. So nurture your existing social circle and gradually expand it even if it's just one person now. Aim for quality, not quantity. We live in the age of instant gratifications, and while we may be able to make instant 'friends' on Facebook or other social media platforms, these friends are really just acquaintances. Real friendships take time and effort to cultivate.

5. **Consider coaching or therapy.** If your loneliness is debilitating or ongoing and it's not improving, it may be time for you to seek professional support. It's not a sign of weakness; rather, it's healthy and proactive. With support, you can overcome your sense of unworthiness, rebuild your confidence and change your communication or relationship patterns, and start making genuine and lasting connections.

Finally, remember that there are seven billion people on the planet, so even if the person you are looking for is one in a million, there are still 7,000 candidates. So get out there – don't be the best kept secret!

4. Finding Your Courage

I am an old man and I have known a great many troubles,
but most of them never happened.
  – Mark Twain

F.E.A.R.

What is fear? Simply put, it's the feeling caused by an impending danger, real or imagined. Notice that I said real *or* imagined, since often fear only lives in our imagination, and is subjective and self-generated, rather than objective and real. Hence, fear is also known as *False Evidence Appearing Real* (F.E.A.R).

A relevant idea to bring in here is that of the 'comfort zone'. We often hear that we should go out of our comfort zone, and we know that we will feel uncomfortable or afraid when we do it. That's why it's called the comfort zone! Every time we step outside it and do something new or significant, our fear comes along for the ride too.

By the way, you may have not heard that there are two more zones outside the comfort zone: the 'stretch zone' and 'panic zone'. As the names suggest, stretch zone is where you stretch yourself and where growth occurs, while panic zone is where you are overstretched and you get into a panic.

The panic zone is where we tend to get into when we go through a breakup or divorce. Our intimate relationship is closely tied to our identity, and we care about it so much that 'failing' it often leads to a crisis. It triggers all our insecurities and we find ourselves in a state of panic, either consciously or unconsciously.

One of our greatest fears about breakups is the emotional storm that we will have to experience – the raw, messy, painful feelings that will overwhelm us and from which we may never be able to fully recover. The loss of control is frightening. (I have covered the do's and don'ts in riding the emotional storm in **chapter two**, so check it out if you haven't already done so.)

Another great fear is about our future, or the lack thereof. We think that we are 'broken' and unloveable, so we are afraid we will never love or be loved again, or we will never find someone better than our ex and we will be alone for the rest of our lives. And that's a frightening prospect.

First of all, we need to understand that fear is a defence mechanism, protecting us from danger by getting us ready to fight or flee, so we should learn to embrace it.

Even if you are not ready to embrace it right now, at least give yourself permission to be afraid rather than avoid or deny it. After all, it's doing what it's supposed to do.

We are constantly co-creating our lives with fear, and the moment we stop feeling afraid is the moment we stop learning and growing as a person.

Fear isn't a monster. It's a feeling, and just like any feeling it will pass. Giving yourself permission to feel afraid will allow it to flow unhindered *through* you and then dissipate; avoiding or denying it will only build up its intensity over time until you are driven by nothing but fear.

Also, as we mentioned in **chapter two**, the trick in dealing with fear – and other negative emotions – is to acknowledge it while at the same time not wallowing in it or reacting to it, as the latter will only magnify it. It's like the difference between feeling nervous about doing something new (normal reaction) versus having an anxiety attack because of it (over-reaction). Don't turn your fear from a normal reaction into an over-reaction.

Confidence is Overrated

Personally, I think confidence is overrated. I know this is a strong statement to make, but I'm ready to back it up.

First, just like fear, confidence is a feeling. And, like most feelings, it's fleeting and mostly outside our control. That's why some days we wake up feeling like we are on top of the world, while on other days we feel so crap that we can't even get out of bed. Or we may feel confident in one area of our lives while utterly deflated in another. That lack of consistency means we cannot rely on it during our breakup recovery, when we need all the mental and emotional strength we can muster.

Another problem with confidence is that we believe we either have confidence or we don't, so a fortunate few seem to be born with an abundance of it while the rest of us mere mortals struggle to 'fake it till you make it'. This is such a disempowering belief and it doesn't give the majority of us a fair chance at dealing with our fears.

Confidence is also meant to be based on our achievements in the past, so presumably we are supposed to feel more confident as we accumulate more accolades or as we get older and wiser. So we work our butt off and keep waiting and waiting for the day when we wake up feeling confident. Of course, that day never comes.

Think about it: if confidence is the result of our past achievements, then working on improving our confidence without first having achieved anything is completely futile. It's like building castles in the air.

Instead, we should work on accumulating our achievements first. The problem with that, however, is that it would lead us straight into the common trap of confusing our self-worth with our external circumstances or achievements (which I will discuss in **chapter six**).

Courage

> *Courage doesn't always roar. Sometimes it's a quiet voice at the end of the day saying, 'I'll try again tomorrow.'*
> – Mary Anne Radmacher
> *Lean Forward into Your Life*

Unlike confidence, courage is an attitude or mindset, and therefore within our control and far more useful. **It's an *act of will* that we can all perform at any moment from now on, even if we have failed every step of the way in the past.**

Moreover, it doesn't need to be something extraordinary, as we can carry out small acts of courage across different areas of our lives every single day. It's not about faking it until you make it. Instead, it's about building a valuable skill or virtue over time.

Second, while confidence is linked to success (whatever your definition of it may be), there are other more important factors contributing to it. If you talk to people, in particular women, who have 'made it' in their field, you will discover that many of them are still lacking in confidence and plagued by fears and self-doubt, thinking they are a fraud or an imposter.

Knowing this can be very comforting for the rest of us. For them, it's not about having more confidence, but listening to their fears and inner critic less (we will cover the inner critic in **chapter five**), and acting in spite of their fears. **They have taken massive action to get to where they are today while being afraid all the time.** Isn't that the very definition of courage?

By relying on their will and untangling their feelings from their actions, they took action when they were scared and unsure, or when they just didn't 'feel like it'. In other words, they felt the fear but acted from courage.

It's a myth that we can't be brave or courageous when we are afraid. I would argue that it's the *only time* we can be brave!

For example, if someone is gifted in public speaking, every time he or she goes to speak in public, they merely express their talent or strength. However, for someone like myself who has no natural talent in public speaking, each time I bring myself to talk in front of a group, it is an act of courage (and a little like pulling teeth, incidentally). And I've performed many, many acts of courage – by choice or not!

What I've learned is that the more you face fear and do the things you think you cannot do, the easier the rest of your life becomes. Conversely, if you run away from what you are afraid of today, you will still have to come back and face it tomorrow, so why not just get it over and done with? Then tomorrow you will be equipped to face even bigger challenges and greater fears.

Finally, you are never done! Courage is a daily practice, like taking showers or brushing your teeth. The good news is that you don't have to perform herculean acts in order to build up that muscle of courage. Just small acts of courage regularly are sufficient.

Strategies

> *Life begins at the end of your comfort zone.*
> – Neale Donald Walsch

Because fear is such a strong emotion, most of the time it's easy to notice when we are scared – even for those of you who are not accustomed to feeling your feelings. And that's good news. Awareness is the first step to change. That said, sometimes fear appears in our lives in disguise, in particular as comparison, perfectionism and procrastination. Let us look at a few strategies that can help us manage fear and some of its disguises.

1. Change your relationship with fear

Do not see fear as your enemy. Instead, learn to embrace your fear rather than try to get rid of it. In any case, it's not possible to become 'fearless', despite what some personal development gurus would have you believe. You will be scared, unless you always stay inside your comfort zone.

Part of embracing your fear means that you recognise it for what it is – a natural, self-defence mechanism. So don't blame yourself for or feel bad about feeling scared. Instead, remind yourself that fear has good intentions. Bring in some self-compassion and soothe yourself as if you were a small child or your best friend.

2. Stay calm and objective

Remember the quote at the start of this chapter? Most of the troubles we imagine never come to pass. So remind yourself of the reality, not your imagined worst case scenarios.

Fears about breakups are very common – in particular fears around not being able to fully recover from the heartbreak and the prospect of living a lonely, loveless existence after a breakup or divorce. The reality, however, is that **an overwhelming majority of people manage to heal from their breakups and go on to have new and more satisfying relationships,** *provided* they are willing to learn the lessons their previous relationships have to teach.

It's not always easy, though. Our mind plays tricks on us when we are scared, and we imagine the worst case scenarios and then feel like we have too much to lose. Every little setback triggers our insecurities. (This is where *emotional resilience* comes in, which we talked about at length in **chapter two**.)

For now, remember fear isn't a monster. It's a feeling. And just like any feeling, it will pass if we allow room for it, to feel it and to sit 'in the fire' with it. However, we typically do two things: we either avoid it and thereby intensify it over time, or we react (*or* over-react) by turning to behaviours that are often unhelpful if not downright destructive to try to stop it, such as reaching out to our ex for assurance or stalking them.

3. Avoid the comparison trap

As social creatures, it's completely normal to want to compare ourselves with those around us because we want to make sure that we are doing okay compared to our peers. However, we often compare our 'insides' with other people's 'outsides', and we wonder why they look like they have it all together while we struggle to just get through the day. It makes us feel inadequate and so alone when we look at only the highlight reels of other people's lives. As the saying goes, "compare despair."

This is especially true during the post-breakup period. With social media so prevalent in our lives, we end up getting hurt when we 'accidentally' see pictures on Facebook of our ex having a great time or even starting a new relationship with other people.

It also makes us feel that they have moved on all too soon, while we are still stuck in the past. Regardless of whether that is true or not, it's still enough to ruin our day (or week) while we obsess about it and what it all *means*.

One effective way to overcome this is to set yourself up for success. By that I mean be hyper-vigilant about what and who you surround yourself with, online and offline. So stop reading fashion magazines, unsubscribe from unhelpful emails or newsletters, and hide your Facebook newsfeeds from family and friends who project an image of perfection. Be on your own side. Get on with your own life and focus on your own healing.

4. Be an imperfectionist

Here's a secret: *you are never ready! And you will never 'feel like it', or be 'good enough'.* Avoid the all-or-nothing mindset of a perfectionist. When we try to wait until we are perfect and ready, it stops us from going after what we want, be it a new relationship, a new job, or a new life after our breakup or divorce. And the gap between where we are and where we want to be seems insurmountable. No wonder we feel stuck!

A good way to get unstuck is to give yourself permission to be human (*not* super-human), and to take constant baby steps rather than trying to go for dramatic makeovers and get discouraged when things don't work out straight away. **Indeed, give yourself permission to do things badly and slowly while scared.** It's so liberating that you'd find yourself getting more done and making greater progress than if you did with a perfectionist mindset.

5. Choose courage

By now, you've all heard that courage is about acting in spite of fear. Or, as they say, 'feel your fear but do it anyway.' It's a *choice*: choosing action in alignment of your goals and values instead of acting out of fear and other negative feelings.

Know that your feelings are fleeting and are not inherently good or bad or even scary, and learn to detach from them. By untangling your feelings from your actions, you can choose to take brave actions despite your fears and self-doubt. In other words **you can be shit scared, but act in the opposite way.** Your feelings are signals: they contain valuable information, but they are *not* instructions so you don't have to act on them.

Also, remember action often comes *before* clarity and confidence, not after. The loop goes like this: courage > action > clarity and confidence. Courage is like a muscle and requires daily practice to flex that muscle, so act before you *feel* ready. Choose courage moment-to-moment to build your confidence and momentum, then the momentum will carry you through the long term.

At the risk of sounding super cheesy, there is another acronym of fear: *Face Everything And Rise.* Are you ready to face your fear and rise?

The Power of Vulnerability

No discussions on courage would be complete without talking about vulnerability.

We hear about it a lot these days. It has become one of the buzzwords ever since writer and researcher Brené Brown's TED talks on shame and vulnerability went viral. But what does vulnerability look like for those of us after a breakup, separation or divorce?

For me, it simply means opening up to others what is hard for us to share. Often this means our feelings – especially negative ones – and fears, but it could also be our childhood wounds, family secrets or anything else we keep hidden out of shame or guilt.

As children, we could be as open and vulnerable as we liked. Yet as adults, we become more closed and less trusting, especially after we've been hurt or betrayed a few too many times. We decide that vulnerability *is* weakness. So we put up walls around our heart and put on masks to keep us safe.

This is not just in romantic relationships. Many of us find that as we get older, we seem to have fewer and fewer close friends. Apart from the hustle of our modern lives, one important reason is that we are less willing to be open and vulnerable. Or we wait for the other person to be vulnerable first, and it becomes a waiting game.

Being vulnerable and showing your soft underbelly is hard, but the benefits are so worth it. By being vulnerable, we create more intimate and richer connections with people in our lives, **as well as a sense of safety in the danger of sharing our deepest fears, wounds and secrets.** It's a paradox. As an added bonus, most of the time vulnerability breeds vulnerability.

I believe that true vulnerability requires strength and courage. It takes guts to open your heart and to give and receive love. After all, there are no guarantees in life and in love. We don't know if the person we give our love to is worthy of our love, or if our love will ever be reciprocated. What if we get hurt again? When we do get hurt, which happens from time to time, it takes strength to know when to ask for support, and courage to ask for it.

As Brené Brown says, "vulnerability sounds like truth and feels like courage. Truth and courage aren't always comfortable, but they're never weakness."

So how do we regain that sense of child-like trust and be more open and vulnerable?

1. Shift your mindset

One of the biggest barriers to vulnerability is that our (Western) culture teaches us that it's weak to be 'needy', and strong people meet their own needs, **so we mistake independence for strength**

and vulnerability for weakness. However, as I mentioned earlier, true vulnerability requires strength and courage. It takes tremendous guts to open our hearts and trust again, as well as to ask for support when we need it.

2. Manage your risks

Another big barrier to vulnerability is our fear of getting hurt by being vulnerable with the wrong people, and that's a valid concern. It's not realistic or safe to just drop all of our defences and make ourselves dangerously vulnerable. After all, we all deserve protection.

Instead, I encourage you to discern what protection you actually need from all the extra armour we put on. It's a process to re-learn who and how to trust again. It's about finding the right people and speaking your truth to the 'ears that can hear you' – as one of my favourite podcasters like to say – even if it is just one person to start with.

3. Open up little by little

It follows from the last suggestion that you don't have to be completely vulnerable overnight, especially if you have been badly hurt or if the betrayal happened recently. It's normal to go through a period of intense distrust when we decide to close our hearts permanently. After all, **we have a tendency to see a problem and think that the solution is the exact opposite.**

So take your time to regain your sense of trust. Start where the stake is low; for example, be honest when you are having a bad day, instead of automatically replying, "I'm fine" to every "How are you?" Share bit by bit until you become more comfortable with being vulnerable, then you can share even more, provided you are satisfied that the person has earned your trust.

4. Trust yourself

Often our lack of trust in others is intrinsically linked to our distrust in ourselves – we don't think we are able to deal with another hurt or betrayal if things go wrong. However, **we forget that as human beings, we are incredibly adaptable and resilient; we can bounce back quicker than we think we could.**

This is especially true if you go into any new relationship or experience with a *growth* mindset. When you are willing to grow from each and every experience, it'd be great if things work out. If they don't, you learn something valuable anyway. Either way, you can't lose.

5. Have faith in the universe

Ok, this one is a bit 'woo-woo' and that's why I saved it for last. Even if you don't have enough faith in yourself and other people, know that whatever happens you will be ok, and that you are being held and supported by the universe. How do I know this? Well, you are here now, aren't you? It took enough people to love and support you and all the right circumstances for you to exist here today.

At the end of the day, vulnerability allows us to recognise that we can't do it alone and we need others; it gives us a healthy sense of humility and, yes, faith.

5. Overcoming Your Inner Critic

It's not what you say out of your mouth that determines your life, it's what you whisper to yourself that has the most power.
  – Robert T. Kiyosaki

Meet Mr. or Mrs. Negative

We all seem to have a special talent for finding critical things to say about the world, about others and especially about ourselves. Our inner chatter gets even louder when we are going through a rough time. It triggers our deepest insecurities, and all we see are our faults and nothing else.

Why? It's easy to just go with the flow when things are going well, but the minute we make a mistake, hit a setback, or, God forbid, fail – like when we 'fail' a relationship or marriage – we pounce on ourselves and beat ourselves up. Talk about kicking ourselves while we are down! **We abandon ourselves, precisely when we need to be on our own side the most.**

The most common way for us to judge and beat ourselves up is through our inner critic, which is that negative voice inside all of our heads. It can be downright nasty and mean, and says things like, *You are stupid and pathetic!* or it can be more subtle like, *Don't be naive. It's not possible to bounce back better than before.*

It consists of negative messages such as criticisms, judgments and rules that you have received throughout your life from many external sources, ranging from your family, friends and partner (including ex-partners) to the media and the broader culture. It *thinks* it is protecting you and keeping you safe from failure by resisting change. After all, if you don't try, you won't fail, right?

While the inner critic may have served you well in the past, it is now holding you back. It makes up stories or even lies about who you are and what you do, including all your *perceived* weaknesses, mistakes and other imperfections. And the worst part is its moral judgment and shame.

Because we have received these messages throughout our lives, those messages have been *internalised* over time. In other words, they have become a part of us, automatically or even unconsciously. This is especially the case if we received the messages as kids because we had few filters and we trusted our parents or other caregivers, so we took everything on board.

> As a kid, I took on board the message that I was stubborn and strong-willed. My parents joked about how my future husband would have a hard time with a wife like me.
>
> While these days I choose to see myself as patient and determined, my inner critic went to town with this message after my breakup. I kept thinking that, because of my stubbornness and strong will, my ex found me hard to 'manage' and preferred the company of some other woman who was softer and more submissive. While my rational mind knew it was nonsense, my inner critic kept repeating the same message until I started to believe that maybe it was all my fault and I had pushed him away.

It's likely that your inner critic is also doing a great job of beating you up with questions such as *What's wrong with me?*, *What did I do wrong?* or *Why wasn't I enough?* and comes up with answers such as, *Maybe I'm not pretty enough, I nagged too much* or *We didn't have sex enough.*

In addition to these external messages, most of the thoughts we generate internally every day are also negative. This is due to the nature of our thoughts and our hardwired 'negativity bias'. As a result, our inner critic behaves like a broken record, latching onto our worst fears and endlessly generating negative thoughts and feelings such as *I wasn't enough* or *I'm unloveable.*

Indeed, the real power of the inner critic lies in *repetition*. Whenever we have heard, repeated and internalised the same things to ourselves so much they feel true, we stop questioning what our inner critic says to us and start believing in all its nonsense.

> Towards the end of our relationship, my ex was calling me all kinds of names, but what really landed for me was when he called me a demanding bitch. At first I was having none of it because I knew I gave him a lot of space in our relationship – as I'd always done in my previous relationships – and he was just trying to hurt me. However, after being called that regularly for months, I started to doubt myself and I thought maybe he was right after all and I was indeed a demanding bitch. This incident really drove home to me that something that has no basis in reality can appear real when it's repeated often enough.

Triggers: Inner Critic on Fire

Comparison is the thief of joy.
– Theodore Roosevelt

So why are we so dissatisfied with ourselves?

One fun little fact first: according to research studies, we have up to *70,000 thoughts per day*, and about eighty to ninety per cent of these thoughts are repetitive. In other words, we are thought machines, and we are stuck in the same thought patterns day in day out. It's fine to think a negative thought seven times a day, but when we ruminate over it 700 times a day, we have a problem.

On top of this fun little fact, we human beings also have a neurological preset called the 'negativity bias'. Our brains are hardwired to pay more attention and react more quickly and strongly to negative than to positive news. Good evolutionary reasons exist for this negativity bias, as negative events – pain, illness, injury, or even death – can be much more costly in survival terms than positive events.

So combining the two facts above, most of our daily 70,000 thoughts are negative and they have been repeated everyday of our lives. **We bombard ourselves with negativity all day long.**

I don't know about you, but that's rather depressing and it seems we are basically living in our own private hell. No wonder we are our own worst enemy!

And that's not all: in addition to our biology, there are other factors or 'triggers' contributing to our self-critical tendencies. We might be doing okay on most days of our healing journey, but when we are triggered, all of a sudden we find ourselves in a deep, dark pit of self-loathing and despair. There are no better ways to prepare yourself by learning to recognise, and then remove, reduce or replace those triggers.

Here are two of the most common triggers:

1. Comparisons

We are social creatures and we crave social approval. We want to be liked, to belong, to fit in; that means knowing how we are doing compared to those around us, so we can adjust our positions accordingly.

However, with easy access to our peers' lives on social media today, we are inundated by information that has been heavily edited. We end up 'comparing and despairing', when we compare our 'insides' with other people's 'outsides', and wonder why others have it all together while we fall short by comparison.

Rather than looking inward and appreciating our unique talents and strengths, we look externally for validation. And when we don't get it, we turn on ourselves with harsh self-criticism.

2. Perfectionism

Perfectionism is the refusal to accept any standard short of perfection, often caused by having unrealistic expectations or a fear of mistakes.

Perfectionism naturally leads to self-judgment and self-criticism; when you have impossibly high standards, it doesn't take much to fall short of those standards and beat yourself up subsequently.

Alternatively, you won't even try because you believe you don't have the skills or resources to do it perfectly, so why bother? And guess what? You have another excuse to criticise yourself harshly for being lazy, scared or not 'having what it takes'. So you are doomed if you try, and you are doomed if you don't.

Impacts

First of all, obviously there is the emotional impact of hurt and pain. Imagine being called stupid repeatedly by your own parents and then internalising that message for many years. Or imagine being told that you are stubborn and men would have a hard time being with you.

Also, I've observed two seemingly opposite behaviours in my clients. They can become overachievers, constantly trying to improve, perform, perfect and people-please. This is what I consider to be a fight response when we are under stress. On the other hand, they may become paralysed and end up avoiding, procrastinating or isolating themselves from others, which is the flight or freeze response. Sometimes they will swing between the two responses depending on the situation.

For example, some women may throw themselves into their work after a breakup or divorce to distract themselves from their inner chatter about their 'failed' relationship. Others may choose to focus on their kids and become overly involved in their lives to ease the parenting guilt their inner critic makes them feel. Some may over-exercise or go on strict diets in order to stop their inner critic from berating their body or comparing their body to that of a younger woman. Remember, the inner critic loves to 'compare and despair'.

However, there are also more serious consequences. Some people may engage in addictions or other self-destructive habits such as drugs, alcohol, food and shopping in order to avoid or numb themselves. While some of these habits are more socially acceptable than others, they are still addictions and may cause more serious problems in the long term.

Strategies

> *Our own worst enemy cannot harm us as much as our unwise thoughts. No one can help us as much as our own compassionate thoughts.*
> – Buddha

How do we overcome this deadly combo of external messaging, negative rumination, comparison and perfectionism that feeds our incessant negative self-talk? In particular, our negativity bias is strong, as we are designed by nature to spot possible danger or threat. Therefore, we need to make a few conscious efforts to overcome it.

1. Shift your mindset

First of all, remember your inner critic for what it is. Instead of seeing it as the enemy and somehow abnormal, it's a *normal* and *natural* part of the human psyche, which protects us from getting hurt either physically or emotionally by keeping us in our comfort zone and not taking any risks – and so not making any mistakes. Therefore, it has good intentions.

However, the way it goes about trying to keep us safe – by being negative, critical, or downright mean and derogatory – is often counter-productive and ends up keeping us scared and small.

A great way to see your inner critic is like an over-protective parent. We need to explain and ease their anxiety with kind, good-humoured patience rather than target it as the enemy and trying to resist it at all costs.

2. Try a three-step process

a) Notice your negative self-talk

Awareness, or mindfulness, is the first step to change. As they say, seeing is freeing. The tricky part about self-talk is that we've repeated it so many times before that it ends up feeling *true*. Also, it has become automatic and it's not always easy to catch ourselves 'in the act', especially at the start.

An effective trick is to use your *feelings* as your cue. Whenever you become aware you are feeling anxious, depressed, angry or upset during your breakup journey, use this as your signal to *pause* and reflect on your thoughts. In other words, stop yourself when you have a negative thought and instead think, *Wait… that's just my inner critic*. Sometimes merely identifying and labelling it is enough for your inner critic to lose its power.

Then, assess it objectively and hopefully with lots of self-love and curiosity, not harsh criticism or judgment. **Love and curiosity are the antidote to judgment.**

Ask yourself: *What's the intention and/or the truth behind it?* This process is like peeling onions, so keep asking yourself the same questions until you find the gold nugget. It will take a while to get to the truth if you are new to it.

> For example, I run workshops, Meetups and other events for my coaching practice. As a recovering perfectionist and still a huge introvert to this day, I never feel quite ready with them. My inner critic usually has a field day and it will

bombard me with negative chatter such as *You don't have what it takes, You've got nothing interesting or useful to say*, or *People don't want to hear what you have to say anyway.* Ouch!

So I would put myself through this process:

What's my intention? I want to make sure I start the preparation early and do a good job.

Why? Because I care and I want everyone to get as much value out of my events as possible.

And what's the truth? The truth is that I am a busy life coach, business owner, wife and mum, and my tendency is to always over-prepare no matter what!

Over time, you can observe the words and phrases in your negative self-talk, as they often are repetitive and boring like a broken record. You will start to spot common patterns and triggers.

For example, my inner critic was pretty loud when I was writing this book. However, because I recognised its familiar refrains such as *Who do you think you are?* and *You don't have what it takes* straight away, it had very little power over me.

As you become better at noticing your inner critic, it's helpful to remember that we are *not* our thoughts or our feelings. We are so much more, so be mindful of them – but don't over-identify or fuse with them. This is where the second step of the process comes in.

b) Disengage from your inner critic

Because the inner critic tries to present it as the truth, the key is to see your inner critic as *separate* from you, and that, moreover, it doesn't define you. So, after you catch yourself talking rubbish to yourself in the first step, the next step is to disengage or dis-identify from it. In other words, you acknowledge it but you don't buy into it.

Mantras and affirmations are particularly useful here when you are in the grips of your inner critic. Here are a few examples of what you can say to your inner critic when you are under attack:

- *Thanks for sharing, but I've got this*. Remember that your inner critic is just trying to help, albeit in a clumsy way, so thank it, but show you are in charge, instead of being defensive or combative.
- *There's a thought or That's an interesting thought, I'll get back to you*. Acknowledge your inner critic but don't indulge in it; be firm and friendly, or even playful.
- *I don't agree with that or Let's just agree to disagree*. When your inner critic gets really noisy, just agree to disagree and move on. Don't waste energy and time to try to prove it wrong.

c) Shift your focus and move on

It's been said that our attention is like a combination *spotlight* and *vacuum cleaner*: it illuminates what it rests upon and then sucks it into your brain. So be careful where you place your attention or focus!

Shifting your focus is like changing the tracks on your record. There are a number of ways you can do it, such as shift it to your breathing, physical movements, music or other positive distractions, and then just go on with the rest of your day. The idea is not to react automatically to your inner critic and spiral down with chocolate (or whatever your vice is) to make yourself feel better.

I particularly like to ask powerful questions. The quality of your questions determines the quality of your life. When you ask yourself shitty questions like *What's wrong with me?* or *Why can't I keep my man/woman?*, your brain goes to work to find answers like *I'm not attractive enough* or *I'm too old*. So ask yourself empowering questions instead, and your brain will go to work for you to find the answers you need to move forward.

You can also substitute your negative self-talk with more positive statements. Instead of using the word 'should' or 'must' that our inner critic loves, like *I should be feeling better by now* or *I must get over my ex*, try 'could' instead, as in *I could be feeling better by now* or *I could get over my ex*. Feel that sense of lightness of possibility, instead of the heaviness of obligation.

Our language is powerful, and being aware of how we use it can either help or hinder our healing process.

3. Be kind to yourself and don't take things too seriously

Your attitude – *how* you do things – is just as important as *what* you do when it comes to outwitting your inner critic. Instead of being at war with yourself, try to be kind toward yourself; forgive yourself for giving yourself a hard time (again!). Know that you did your best and let yourself off the hook.

At the end of the day, ask yourself, *Would I say this to a friend?* If not, don't say it to yourself! Instead of being your worst enemy, make it your mission to be your best friend. **We often abandon ourselves when we need to be our friend the most.** (We will cover a lot more on befriending ourselves in **chapter six**.)

Also, when you get to know your inner critic better, you will start to notice that its tone is heavy, serious and humourless. So the more lighthearted you can be about something, the less likely your inner critic will be able to attack you. There's a reason why we don't hear our inner critic when we are having fun and laughing!

4. Take baby steps

Be very, very patient with yourself. Kind, good-humoured patience is the name of the game. It takes months, if not years, of practice to be able to catch yourself 'in the act' and then to shift from negative to positive self-talk.

If last month you were able to catch yourself one out of twenty occasions, and this month you are able to do it two out of twenty occasions, that's a win! It's not so much about how fast you shift as the fact you shift, so just keep going and don't give up.

It's like learning a new language. How many of us studied a foreign language in school and still speak it? Not many. Yes, we went to class once or twice a week, did the homework, and studied for the exams. But that wasn't enough. We needed to practise it the rest of the time and we didn't.

Learning positive self-talk is like learning a new language – you need to practise constantly until you become fluent in it.

5. Get support

Last but not least, don't struggle on your own and beat yourself up for beating yourself up! Get support, especially if your inner critic is out of control, chronic and pervasive that it undermines your self-esteem and wellbeing.

Try Self-Approval Today

> *You've been criticising yourself for years and it hasn't worked. Try approving of yourself and see what happens.*
> Louise Hay
> *You Can Heal Your Life*

Instead of criticising and berating yourself, you will feel more happy, peaceful and confident if you choose to practice positive self-talk. It will also help shield you from the criticisms and judgments of others.

Don't underestimate the power of your self-talk. Changing your inner dialogue to be more loving toward yourself will change your life.

6. Falling in Love with Yourself

If you want to see the love of your life, look in the mirror.
  – Byron Katie,
  Loving What Is: Four Questions That Can Change
  Your Life

Radical Self-Love

In the aftermath of a breakup or divorce, we need self-love and self-compassion more than ever before.

Right now your job isn't to love someone else; it is just to love yourself. Radically. Fiercely. Unconditionally. Like you've never loved yourself before.

We all crave to be loved and cared for, but we are not willing to give that to ourselves. Instead, we look outside ourselves for love and for someone else to 'complete' us, not realising that our greatest source of love resides within us. *Nobody can complete us because we are already complete.*

Yes, we *want* someone to complement us and bring more fulfilment into our lives, but we don't *need* them to make our life full. As mentioned earlier, it's never about getting the love from outside – it's an *inside job* all along. Everything starts from within.

Indeed, the lack of self-love can leave us with a bottomless void that can never be filled by another person. When we don't love ourselves, we are always looking for someone else to do it for us, hoping the unloved part of us will finally feel loved; we are demanding from others the love we aren't giving to ourselves. And we wonder why we don't get it! We are the only ones who can fill that void with self-love.

We are so afraid of being alone that we put up with being disrespected in a relationship; we are so afraid of being abandoned that we end up abandoning ourselves.

What's great about self-love is that it has a very feminine energy. It's gentle, soothing and comforting like a loving parent's embrace. It validates our pain and our difficulties. On the other hand, courage gives us the fierce masculine energy that motivates us into action despite our fears and other negative emotions. **We need both kindness and fierceness. It's like the yin and the yang.**

In this chapter we will discuss what self-love is, some common misconceptions of it, and how to be more loving towards ourselves, especially when we are facing a breakup or divorce.

Wholehearted Acceptance

To be yourself in a world that is constantly trying to make you something else is the greatest accomplishment.
– E. E. Cummings

We hear about self-love a lot these days, but many people are confused about what it is and how it looks like in practice, or they think that it's rather 'woo-woo' and therefore not for them.

I see self-love as the *wholehearted acceptance of things as they are* – as opposed to wishing they were different. This includes accepting who you are and where you are on your life's journey, and by that I mean *all* of you and your life, the good, the bad and the ugly.

It's about embracing yourself as you are, warts and all, and from that solid foundation you can work towards becoming even better, rather than thinking that there is something wrong with you and you need to 'fix' yourself.

Self-love is the key to living your most amazing life, and is the cure that allows you to let go of perfection and release self-judgment. It's also the antidote to your inner critic and it will set your true self free.

Why is that? Because acceptance is the opposite of judgment. As we saw in **chapter five**, the inner critic is all about judgment, and it wants to deny rather than accept reality. Its weapons of choice are either obligation and guilt (all your 'shoulds'), or fear and self-doubt.

Another big part of acceptance is forgiveness: forgiving yourself and others when things go wrong – and they will – over and over again. (More on this in **chapter eight**).

The Most Important Relationship

To love oneself is the beginning of a life-long romance.
– Oscar Wilde

The self-love journey is fundamentally about changing your relationship with yourself. On this journey you will learn that it is the most important relationship you will ever have in your life.

You are the common denominator in all your life's ups and downs, and you are with yourself 24/7 while other people come in and out of your life.

Therefore, don't delegate to others the responsibility to be on your own side and to love yourself unconditionally. When you realise your self-love is *the* source of love in your life, and give it to yourself no matter what, you will feel like that you have finally come home to yourself. **In fact, loving yourself is like coming full circle after you have been looking for love everywhere else, often in all the wrong places.**

In *The Alchemist,* the shepherd boy Santiago dreamed of a treasure and set off in search of it. As it turned out, the treasure that he had been looking for was buried in the ruins where he had the dream in the first place. It was there all along and all it took was for him to rediscover it.

Self-love is like that. You already have it inside of you and all you have to do is to rediscover it. Isn't that an empowering realisation?

If you want to dig a little deeper, self-love is made up of three elements according to my favourite self-compassion expert Kristin Neff.

1. Self-kindness

We behave with gentleness and kindness towards ourselves and we affirm to ourselves that *we are enough*.

It is the opposite of self-judgment, self-criticism, perfectionism and comparison. I prefer to think of this as experiencing a feeling of *sweetness* towards ourselves, as if we were a friend or a small child. What it looks like in reality means speaking and behaving kindly to ourselves, and we forgive ourselves when things go wrong.

2. Common humanity

Often we forget as human beings we are imperfect and prone to making mistakes. We are all connected in our suffering, or as I like to say, *we are all screwed up!*

By focusing on the common humanity that connects us all rather than the differences that divide us, we feel we are not alone and our struggles are universal struggles. It then becomes easier to let go and accept ourselves and our situation as it is.

This element of self-love gives us not only a broader perspective, but also gives us permission to be ourselves and feel okay because we are normal, rather than feel like a loser or a freak. Then we are less likely to fall into the comparison trap where we compare our insides with other people's outsides and believe they 'have it all together'.

3. Mindfulness

By paying attention to the here and now, we are more likely to catch ourselves when we fall victim to self-judgment and self-criticism, and to take steps to bring in self-compassion to help restore the balance. At the same time, we don't ignore or exaggerate our suffering; we simply notice it as we move to comfort ourselves immediately.

This is especially valuable when things go wrong because of our negative reactions. After all, when things are fine, we are just cruising along in life. What this looks like in reality is that we are able to notice and validate our underlying feelings and needs, and take time out to process them *in the moment* with lots of self-love and forgiveness, as opposed to dealing with them in hindsight, or not dealing with them at all.

> As a recovering perfectionist, this is a topic close to my heart. I used to be extremely hard on myself and my inner critic wouldn't shut up. I was very motivated to do more and be more, but the motivation came from a place of fear and scarcity – *I'm not smart enough* or *What would other people think?* – rather than a place of love and abundance, which has thoughts like *I know enough* and *I'll be fine no matter what others think*.
>
> So even though I managed to be productive and achieve most of the goals I set for myself, I didn't feel any lasting joy and satisfaction with my achievements, and I was constantly striving for the next set of goals in order to 'improve' myself.
>
> In other words, I kept moving my own goal posts. My to-do list was endless and constantly growing. Deep down, I felt there was something fundamentally wrong with me and I needed to be fixed. It wasn't until I had a good grasp of what self-love was that I began to shift towards accepting myself regardless of what I got done (or didn't).
>
> And self-love came to my rescue again after my devastating breakup. Instead of beating myself up for and blaming the breakup on all my not-enoughness, I decided I was worth

my own love, and I cut myself a massive amount of slack. I took really good care of myself, stayed physically active while at the same time had plenty of rest. And I gave myself permission to grieve and to cry whenever I felt like it instead of stuffing it all down.

Rebuilding Self-Worth

Don't shrink, don't puff up, stand on sacred ground.
– Brené Brown

So far we've explored how to be kinder and more loving to ourselves. Now let's take a look at the other aspect of self-love: becoming the person you love.

This is to do with the idea of self-worth or self-esteem, i.e. how we see or value ourselves. Sadly, many of us value ourselves poorly, and we see ourselves as less than or not enough. It's likely that our self-worth has been slowly eroded over time during a relationship, and then took a huge hit with the breakup or divorce itself.

Our sense of inferiority or inadequacy means we find it hard to even like, let alone love, ourselves. Given our happiness and sense of fulfilment are related to how much we love and accept ourselves, it's little wonder that we feel miserable and unfulfilled.

There are many reasons why we have a low self-worth, and one of the main ones is that we conflate our external circumstances or our goals with our internal self-worth. We think, *I'll be enough when I meet someone special / find my dream job / _____ (fill the blank)*. However, our circumstances and goals are mostly outside our control. It's fine when things are going well or when we achieve our goals, but when things don't go as we have expected, our self-worth inevitably suffers.

For example, our self-worth is usually at all-time low when we've just experienced a breakup or divorce. And it's normal. Even the most confident amongst us will experience a slump in their self-worth.

Nonetheless, people who are able to separate the breakup from their self-worth are better at bouncing back afterwards. They are also more likely to use the experience to help them thrive and choose their next relationship from a place of strength, rather than just survive and settle for less.

By the way, there is nothing wrong with wanting more and better things in our lives. It becomes problematic, however, when we depend on achieving our goals and other things to go our way in order to be happy, not realising that a) we don't always achieve our goals or dreams, and b) **it's nobody else's job to make us happy. They can only make our job easier, but it's still our job at the end of the day.**

Self-love, on the other hand, is inside yourself and therefore within your control. It is not dependent on external circumstances, achievements or other people.

Once you learn how to love yourself *unconditionally* and see yourself as worthy of that love *no matter what*, your self-worth stays intact and remains constant.

Becoming the Person You Love

First, we need to start mentally untangling our self-worth from our external circumstances or goals. In other words, producing thoughts like *my divorce sucks, but I don't suck*, Or, *just because I haven't achieved my goals, it doesn't mean I'm a loser*. Indeed, it's important to look at what you make your negative circumstances or your lack of achievements mean in terms of your self-worth. *And it doesn't have to mean anything.*

Indeed, you are already worthy. **You were loved into being. And just by virtue of being human, you come 'pre-approved'!** No further circumstances, actions or achievements are required.

Therefore, your goals are only for creating more happiness in your life, not to increase your own self-worth.

Many of us think getting our dream partner or our dream job will somehow make us more worthy, so we keep chasing after our next goal or striving to change our circumstances, putting our happiness on hold all the while. However, no amount of external validation will increase our self-worth in the long run; you may enjoy your achievements or praises from others for now, but soon you will be back on the hamster wheel hungry for more.

One of the biggest enemies to self-love as well as to self-worth is our inner critic. We have already discussed it in length in **chapter five**. (If you have skipped the chapter, it would be really useful to go back to find out how we can avoid being our worst enemy.)

For now, just remember that the way we talk to ourselves matters a great deal. Language is how we make sense of ourselves, others and the world. Unfortunately, our muscles for loving self-talk have likely atrophied from years of disuse, so we need to re-condition ourselves with positive, uplifting language in our inner dialogue.

Finally, unlike striving for external circumstances or achievements, every act of self-love and self-care improves our self-worth because it's a message to ourselves that what we need and want matters, and therefore we ourselves are important and worthy.

Common Barriers

If self-love and self-compassion are so vital, why aren't we all more self-loving and kind towards ourselves on a daily basis? The simple answer is that many people are confused about self-compassion.

Here are some of the common misconceptions:

1. We are worried that being loving towards ourselves means we are being selfish, or even narcissistic

This is probably the biggest barrier. As women, we are socially conditioned to be caring and nurturing, and for many of us this means we often put the needs of everyone else before our own. If we don't, then we think we are being selfish (or worried we will be perceived as such by others).

This can't be further from the truth. Self-compassion has our best interests in mind, but it doesn't diminish the interests of others, so we shouldn't confuse it with being selfish. It just means that we take our needs and feelings as seriously as we take those of others, and we don't put ourselves last like a martyr and try to be everything to everyone.

Unless we take good care of ourselves and give ourselves the TLC we need, we run the risk of burnout. We need to fill up our own cup first in order to be there for others. Not to mention that the constant giving may lead to people taking us for granted, and we end up resenting them for it.

I don't know about you, but when I am stressed, sleep-deprived or hungry, I get pretty snarky. On the other hand, when I'm relaxed, well rested and well fed, I'm a joy to be around (if I may say so myself)! *Remember, service doesn't have to mean sacrifice.*

Furthermore, we need to get over what others may think. Yes, some people may feel uncomfortable with our self-loving attitude and practices, but it has nothing to do with us. Given it's the norm that most people are *not* loving towards themselves, we are challenging the status quo and that's bound to strike a nerve in some people. Expect pushbacks and stand your ground. This is where courage and fierceness come in.

2. Some people – in particular, those of us who are high- or over-achievers – are worried that self-love may lead to self-indulgence

However, like a loving but firm parent, self-compassion has our best interests in mind. It doesn't let us off the hook or get away with things that harm us in the long term. For example, instead of being self-indulgent and spending the whole weekend on the couch watching TV and eating junk food, self-compassion would actually gently nudge us to do what's best for our body and mind, even if it is just a walk around the block.

3. Self-compassion makes us lazy and unmotivated

We believe we need to be hard on ourselves in order to become motivated and productive. The (flawed) thinking goes: if we are critical and judgmental with ourselves, this will push us to improve ourselves and overcome our weaknesses, while the reverse will lead to laziness and complacency.

However, using harsh self-criticism and the associated shame and guilt to motivate ourselves may work for a little while, but it will feel horrible. It's also not sustainable and will seriously damage our self-esteem and happiness over time.

Indeed, research has shown that self-criticism diminishes our confidence and motivation, while self-compassion actually contributes to our confidence, motivation and overall wellbeing. Not to mention that when we don't constantly beat ourselves up, it makes our journey much more fun and enjoyable!

Un-Trivialise Self-Care

Now you might be wondering what self-love looks like in daily life, and what the simple self-compassion practices you can do every day.

Self-care is the answer. I see self-care as an expression of self-love, or self-love in action.

The 'traditional' type of self-care that you come across in women's magazines or popular media has been trivialised. It usually centres around pampering or indulging yourself in some sort of binge or splurge, like going on a shopping spree or a luxury holiday. For me, they are only superficial, bandaid fixes.

Real self-care goes much deeper and is about returning to your essence and what truly brings you joy and pleasure. Therefore, they are absolutely *essential* to your wellbeing. Instead of self-indulgence, it's self-preservation. Instead of being just fun and frivolous, there is dignity and fierceness about it. It isn't always sexy or glamorous. In fact, sometimes it can be downright uncomfortable.

So, while self-care can be really simple and doesn't require an expensive price tag, it should be a regular and ongoing practice, not a one-off fix only when you are 'in the mood', or worse, on the brink of a burnout. Also, it's as much about *not* doing as it is about doing.

Indeed, it will require courage on your part to practise it on a regular basis, especially if you are an over-achiever or a people-pleaser, or live in a culture that demands constant performance or conformity from you.

> For example, taking a power nap every day is one of my all-time favourite self-care practices. I used to soldier on without a nap and end up feeling exhausted at the end of the day. Because of the naps, now I feel energised and focused even after a long day. And more productive, too. I used to be reluctant to tell others about it because I sensed that they might think it was self-indulgent. However, now I actively share it with others and encourage them to start taking naps too.
>
> Another one of my self-care practices is having quiet alone time regularly. As an introvert, I need my solitude to rest and recharge my battery in between all my work and social commitments. If I go too long without my alone time, I feel scattered and disconnected from myself, as I get lost in all the 'noise' of the outside world and lose my sense of grounding.
>
> I can't stress enough how important it is to find your own self-care practices, even if it's just one or two things, and make them non-negotiable in your life on a daily or weekly basis.

Real Self-Care

Change your attitude

When it comes to attitude, it's not so much about what you are doing but how you *feel* when you are doing it. Self-care is about honouring yourself as number 1, not last.

So start valuing yourself. Know that you matter and that your feelings and needs matter too. Accept them without self-judgment. What's more, remember that self-love can boost your motivation and productivity much better than harsh self-criticism.

Go back to the basics

When you are new to caring for yourself, go back to the basics. Start with taking care of your physical health through good diet, regular exercise and plenty of rest. Once you've got the hang of the basics, gradually add other self-care activities such as deep breathing, meditation, yoga, journalling, etc.

Also, make sure you schedule time – even just for ten minutes a day. Start small. Consistency trumps intensity, so don't try to meditate for an hour a day and then run out of steam after three days. And whatever you do, never, ever leave it up to chance because, well, life happens; unless you prioritise your self-care, it will get crowded out by your other commitments.

According to John Gottman, a well-known authority on relationships, it's the small things that make or break a marriage. And the motto for their programs is "small things often." Self-love is about our relationship with ourselves, so it's also about the little things we do, or don't do, that either sustains or diminishes it.

Practise positive self-talk

In addition to positive self-talk, you can create and use mantras or affirmations.

Mantras and affirmations are positive, specific words or statements that help you to overcome self-sabotaging, negative thoughts.

Both mantras and affirmations shift your focus from your inner critic's broken record to something much more positive and affirming, and in the process calm your nervous system. However, make sure they actually resonate with you and are believable to you. Many people have mantras or affirmations that they don't believe in and they wonder why they don't work! Some simple, yet powerful mantras or affirmations that I use regularly include:

"Peace."

"I love, accept and forgive myself."

"Today I choose happiness."

"I'm doing the best I can / I did the best I could."

Be patient with yourself

It will take time to rebuild your self-awareness, self-worth and self-love. And it will take time to shift to a new attitude and to adopt new practices where you put yourself first, not last. It's like going to a mental gym and flexing the muscles.

Some days you will feel like you are taking two steps forward then one step backward. What matters is making progress in the right direction, not how fast you get to your destination.

We are all on the journey to becoming more self-loving, myself included. Wouldn't it be the ultimate irony if you beat yourself up for not being self-loving enough?

A Place of Worthiness

Most of us are already skilled at being kind towards others – and that's great news! So let's start using the same skill of compassion on ourselves and give us the love and care we deserve. Instead of being your worst enemy, try to be your best friend.

In closing, I'd like to share with you another one of my cherished quotes from one of my favourite authors:

> *Wholehearted living is about engaging in our lives from a place of worthiness. It's about cultivating the courage, compassion, and connection to wake up in the morning and think, no matter what gets done and how much is left undone, I am enough. It's going to bed at night thinking, yes, I am imperfect and vulnerable and sometimes afraid, but that doesn't change the truth that I am also brave and worthy of love and belonging.*
> *– Brené Brown*
> *The Gifts of Imperfection*

Now over to you:
How much do you value or even know your own needs?

How much self-love and self-care do you practice daily?

7. Finding Ideal Support

If we have no peace, it is because we have forgotten that we belong to each other.
   – Mother Teresa

You Are Not Alone ...

Often when we are going through a breakup or some other difficult life experience, our kneejerk reaction is to withdraw and isolate ourselves. There is definitely a lot of value in spending some quality time alone after a crisis or traumatic event to heal from our wounds, reflect on what has happened and plan for our next move.

However, many people, especially women, stay isolated for too long because they feel embarrassed or even ashamed for having 'failed' in their relationship. They also worry about other people judging, criticising or feeling sorry for them. As a result, they don't keep up with their support network, then they think nobody cares about them.

It also doesn't help that our culture teaches us that it's weak to be 'needy' and that strong people meet their own needs, so *we mistake independence for strength and vulnerability for weakness*. While independence is to be applauded, often we take it too far and try to do everything perfectly on our own.

I've come to believe that there is vulnerability *and* strength in being able to ask yourself, *What do I need?* and then ask others, *Can you help me?* rather than pretending that everything is fine and soldiering on. It takes practice, especially for those of us who are used to being the strong one or the giver.

Reaching out for support is not only a smart move, as **it helps us speed up our healing process; it also allows others to see that they are not alone and to connect with us on a deeper level** of friendship, support and inspiration.

There's nothing like showing our true vulnerability that builds real emotional connection with others. By letting go of the armour that we habitually carry around with us, we give others the permission to let go of theirs too.

After all, we are social creatures, and isolation and loneliness are harmful to our physical, mental and emotional health. Research after research has consistently demonstrated that social interactions are beneficial for *everyone*, even the most shy and introverted amongst us.

> I was one of those independent people. Following my breakup from my ex, at first I was too embarrassed to reach out to my family and close friends for support, especially after I had told everyone that he was 'the one'.
>
> I also thought maybe it was my fault that the relationship fell apart. I didn't want to have to explain myself and I most definitely didn't want anyone's pity. Besides, as an independent and proud woman, I believed (mistakenly) that showing vulnerability was a sign of weakness.
>
> When I eventually did reach out – and started a Meetup community to support other women through difficult breakups and other major life transitions – I realised that my family and friends really did care and were happy to see me making progress and getting back on my feet.
>
> Also, by reaching out I discovered there were many people out there facing similar heartbreaks and feeling lonely and isolated. I wasn't alone! Intellectually, I knew that already – I

couldn't possibly have been the only one struggling. But it wasn't until when I met others in the same boat that I got to witness it for myself firsthand.

In fact, I can't tell you how many times members from my Meetup community came to tell me how much they appreciated hearing other women's stories because it made them feel they were not alone. It's so easy to forget the simple yet profound truth that *we are more alike than different, and we are all in this together.*

On the other hand, when you have isolated yourself for too long, sometimes you become starved for connection. You know how everything tastes great when you are starving? It's the same with relationships. So don't emotionally starve yourself so much that you're willing to settle for anything in a relationship, romantic or not, and ignore all the red flags and boundary violations.

By the way, some people – including those closest to you – may not be able or willing to support you. Don't be discouraged, because they may have a lot on their plate or their own baggage to deal with too. As for those judgmental folks, stay clear of them and remember their judgment says more about them than about you. We will discuss more about how to deal with unhelpful support in the following sections.

Now over to you:
Do you withdraw and stay isolated for too long when going through your breakup or other crises?

What is stopping you from reaching out now?

Unhelpful Support

Most people have no idea what to say to you about your breakup or to support you in your healing, and it's not their fault.

We are not taught how to respond to others who are in distress or going through a tough time. Sometimes we think it's better not to say anything at all. Other times we say too much or the wrong things, and end up imposing our own judgments on others, or worse, hurting them.

Now that you are on the receiving end, you will become acutely aware of how much people fumble through their interactions with you. For example, you will get a lot of bad, unsolicited advice. You will also hear more than once that your ex is 'an asshole' (or substitute their own choice of words), that the breakup is a 'shame' and they are 'sorry' for you.

While this may make you feel better or even understood right now, especially immediately after the breakup, when you are full of righteous indignation and hurt feelings and want to vent to anyone who would listen, it is counterproductive in the long run for your healing journey.

Being seen as an object of pity by your support group, while well-meaning, may reinforce your own belief, consciously or subconsciously, that you are a *victim* and therefore powerless to change your circumstances. Not to mention all the toxic energy it creates around you when you are being seen as a helpless victim, making it harder for you to move on with your life.

Apart from seeing you as a victim, some people in your support group, including those closest to you, may even be critical of you, rather than only of your ex or the breakup. Their judgment and disapproval may be obvious at times while at other times more subtle and covert.

Friends or Foes?

In addition to dealing with unsupportive people within your support group, be prepared to lose some friends. Some common friends will disappear on their own because they feel they have to choose sides due to divided loyalties. It's an unfortunate but common by-product of a breakup or divorce.

Some may even be openly hostile towards you about the choices you have made. Let them be. You can't control how they behave, but you can control how you *react* to their behaviour. Don't feel like you need to explain, defend or justify yourself. Remember to bring in compassion for your former friends – we are all doing the best we can.

On the upside, this may also be an excellent opportunity for you to re-design your inner circle. With those common friends who have remained, you could set boundaries with them so they don't pass on any information on you or your ex, or behave in other inappropriate ways that may leave you in distress or distract you from focusing on your own healing.

Empathy vs. Sympathy

On the other hand, what does helpful support look like? I think empathy plays a big role in this. Empathy is often confused with sympathy, so it's vital to make a clear distinction between the two.

When someone feels sorry for you, they are imagining how awful they would feel if the same thing were to happen to them. In other words, they are bringing their own opinions and judgment to the situation or even to you. Their focus is on what's wrong and what's not working, and they are intent on telling you all about it. This is what sympathy is like.

Most people have no awareness that they are doing you harm by being sympathetic. In fact, sympathetic people are some of the loveliest people you will ever meet. Again, it goes back to the way we have not been taught how to respond to others who are in distress.

Empathy, on the other hand, is about *presence without judgment.* They stand by you, can feel all the intense emotions you are feeling, while at the same time acknowledge your power to change your circumstances and create the life you want. **They see you as a powerful person who is stuck in a bad situation for now, and they trust and support you to get back on your feet.**

People with empathy, not sympathy, are the kind of support you need in a difficult time like this. After all, you are in a particularly vulnerable position and you might temporarily forget the simple yet powerful truth that you are a strong, resilient person with all the inner resources you need to learn from what has happened and to create what you want going forward.

Trust me, you will need to be reminded, over and over, by people who are empathetic to your pain, yet fully acknowledge your power to heal from your past and create a new future you deserve.

> Unfortunately I didn't know the distinction between empathy and sympathy back when I was going through my breakup. As a result, I received a lot of sympathy from well-meaning friends when I confided in them my breakup story. It made me feel very uncomfortable at the time. But I didn't know why, so I just put it down to me being not used to it – being a private, independent person by nature and someone who supported others rather than the other way around.

> However, a deeper reason that I felt uncomfortable – and it only came to me many months after the breakup – was that other people's sympathy made me feel powerless and at the mercy of my circumstances, and I didn't want to feel that way. I had unwittingly cast myself in the role of the victim, while my friends had assumed the role of the rescuer.

> While it wasn't their intention to take away my power and my sense of control, they did just that. So I stopped talking about my story.

> Nowadays, I only share it when I need to explain why I came to life coaching or to provide examples for my clients.

> In my mind, I wasn't a victim, and I never will be.

Teaching People

> *You teach people how to treat you by what you allow, what you stop, and what you reinforce.*
>   – Tony A. Gaskins

How do you stop others from seeing you as a victim and give you the real support you need? You *teach* them how to support you.

There are two ways to go about doing this. First, you can gather around you a new group of empathetic, supportive people who believe in you and want the best for you. It doesn't have to be a big group. In fact, you can start with one, and gradually expand it over time.

Second, you can teach the rest of the people how to treat you, and yes, that includes the 'haters' or the naysayers. Since you can't control what others think, say or do, this means setting boundaries and sticking to them.

1. Nurturing support

Take time to start a support group now if you don't already have one, preferably *before* you have to lean on it for support. That way, you are still in a good headspace to seek out the right people who have your best interests at heart, rather than feeling needy and becoming involved with those who don't.

Keep trying until you find people who are ready to support you the way you want to be supported. Also, consider seeking professional support such as coaching or mentoring if you can't find the kind of support you need in your personal network. You don't have to do it alone.

If you already have a support group, make sure you continue to nurture it over time. While it might sound really obvious, starting and maintaining a support group means spending quality time with the people in your group. Relationships take time. Don't leave it up to chance.

Everyone is busy these days, so if your goal is to build a strong support group, you need to schedule your social time the same way you would schedule your work or doctor's appointments and be 100% committed to them. What gets scheduled gets done.

Also, remember relationships get messy from time to time. More and more people are hiding behind technology to avoid the vulnerability and messiness of real relationships, or simply to avoid the hard work involved. It's far easier to 'like' a post or make a comment on Facebook than to meet and spend time with people face-to-face on a regular basis, or to deal with any dramas that real-life relationships involve.

2. Setting boundaries

As mentioned earlier, judgment and disapproval can come from many directions, and sometimes they may come from those closest to you. This may come as a shock to you, but keep in mind that sometimes those people feel like they can say anything precisely because they are closest to us, not realising that their opinions or judgments are not always welcome.

So it's up to you to allow or not allow certain treatments. This means you actually have to first get clear about how you want to be treated.

For example, if you don't want to be treated like a victim or be criticised for your personal decisions, you can choose to spend less time with the pity party and the self-righteous people. Moreover, boundaries are not reserved for the haters; you can also set boundaries for your friends. One useful boundary is to request them not to pass on any information on you or your ex.

Also, it is vital to remember that **what other people say is more about them than about you**. They don't want to see you struggle because it hurts them or make them feel nervous, but those feelings are about them, not you. So don't take things personally.

It's easier said than done, but I find that while it is very natural that we will take things personally at first, this doesn't mean that we can't then pause, calm ourselves down and look at things more objectively. It will take practice, but it can be done.

When you are ready, talk to them and ask for their understanding and support. Tell them you know they love you or have good intentions, but they are not helping by projecting their fears and worries on you. Do it from a place or love, not defensiveness.

Furthermore, don't get too attached to the outcome. If they understand and can offer you their unconditional support, great. If not, then you have the choice to keep the relationship or to distance yourself from them.

Finally, be patient. You have taught people how to treat you in a certain way, so it will take some time to change that pattern.

Expect pushbacks, as people try to test your boundaries to see how serious you are about them, so don't give up under pressure even if it feels uncomfortable at first. (I will talk more about setting boundaries in **chapter nine**.)

Trust

Your task is not to seek for love, but merely to seek and find all the barriers within yourself that you have built against it.
   – Rumi

When you have lost trust in others, and in men in particular, it takes time to re-learn how and whom to trust.

I believe that when we don't trust others, it's really ourselves whom we don't trust – we don't trust that we can recover from another major heartbreak or even just a simple disappointment, because we've been burned too many times before. We become either easily bruised or overly defensive, and we run away from love and commitment. We choose to either stay single indefinitely, or we settle for lukewarm, half-hearted relationships.

So rebuilding trust in others is really about rebuilding trust in ourselves first and foremost.

First, we need to **forgive ourselves**. Don't beat yourself up for being distrustful. You have closed your heart because it was the right thing to do for self-preservation and it had served you well in the past. However, now you have outgrown the limitation you had placed on yourself.

Second, realise that learning to trust again is **going to be a gradual journey**. We will not wake up one day and find our hearts completely healed and able to trust others again without reservations. It will take time, and it will take work. It's about taking one sometimes painful small step after another to remove all the barriers within yourself that you have built against it.

Third, **be aware of your inner critic**. Try to distinguish your own 'shit' from their issues, and take responsibility to 'keep your side of the street clean', as they say in recovery circles. Don't twist their innocent words or actions or blow things out of proportion.

When we are convinced that people are not trustworthy, we put on the lens and look for evidence to support that belief, while at the same time conveniently overlook anything that is good and decent. What we focus on grows, and negativity breeds negativity.

Of course, it doesn't mean that you throw caution to the wind. Keep your wits about you as you re-learn how and whom to trust. Don't write a person off if they let you down in a small way; at the same time, don't ignore any big red flags or consistent boundary violations. When in doubt, always, always trust your intuition.

Finally, to date and to fall in love again is to **be willing to be burned again**. It's the price we pay for a wholehearted life. The rewards are worth it. We all know that there is no guarantee if you choose – and yes, it's a *choice* – to open your heart and trust again that you will find someone, let alone your soulmate. There are no guarantees in life or in love.

However, you will dramatically increase your probability of finding love again. And with all the inner work that you are doing and will continue to do, this time around you know you will not only be able to survive another heartbreak, but also be stronger and wiser for it.

Sure, there will be fear, but there will also be excitement, hope, passion, possibility and freedom. Which way would you rather live?

We're all just walking each other home.
– Ram Dass

8. Closing the Ex File

If it hurts more than it makes you happy then take the lesson and leave. You will be okay. Some people are only rehearsals for the real thing.
  – Beau Taplin

The Ex File

The process of letting go of your ex and your relationship will not happen overnight. Be patient and give yourself as much self-love and grace as possible. Don't beat yourself up for feeling that you are still not 'over' your ex, or you 'should' not be hurting anymore, especially if you had only just broken up with your ex a few weeks or months ago.

However, if a reasonable amount of time has passed and you feel that you are still sad or angry about the relationship, and you feel stuck now and unable to move forward, or you find yourself attracting similar men, perhaps it's time to close your 'ex file'.

So what is the 'ex file'? It's the hurt feelings, stories, beliefs and other blocks that we still hold onto from our past romantic relationships.

Remember, even though your relationship has ended, there were good parts to the relationship too, or you wouldn't have started it in the first place. Something must have attracted you to your ex. So don't dismiss your ex or the entire relationship as a 'mistake'. Rather than sweeping your last relationship under the carpet, as part of the process of letting go and closing your ex file, it's vital to take a closer look at it.

Better still, instead of looking only at your last relationship, the first step to closing your ex file is to *analyse all your past significant relationships*. Distill the lessons and take them forward with you into your next relationship to make it better.

Here are some powerful questions you can ask yourself when going through each of your past significant relationships:

- What worked?
- What didn't work? What part did you have in why it didn't work?
- What were some of your needs, emotional and otherwise?
- What needs were met? What needs were not met?
- Can you meet your own needs, instead of looking for someone else to meet them?
- What lessons did you learn? What would you do differently?

I'll be the first to admit that this is not going to be a fun exercise, but the beauty of this exercise is to ensure that **you get wiser with each relationship, instead of having the same relationship over and over again with different partners.** Not to mention it provides great insights into yourself and your own needs and wants.

Then, after you have reflected on your past relationships, the second step to closing the ex file is to *find some compassion and forgiveness for your ex*. This is going to be challenging if the relationship didn't end amicably. However, remind yourself that you are doing this for yourself, not for your ex.

I find it to be a game changer for me to remember that people are doing the best they can with whatever they've got.

I also find it a lot easier to find compassion when I remember that most of the time mistakes are not made out of malice, but rather out of carelessness, stupidity or boredom.

We will cover forgiveness in greater details in the next section. For now, a great tool for finding compassion and forgiveness is the practice of **Ho'oponopono** from Hawaii. It consists of four simple yet powerful phrases: *I'm sorry. Please forgive me. Thank you. I love you.*

These words incorporate the power of repentance, forgiveness, gratitude and love. The order is not that important and you can say the words in your head or out loud. Repeat them often or whenever you feel you need to.

The Don'ts

There are certain things that are not helpful in the process of letting go, from the obvious such as stalking – including cyber stalking – to the seemingly innocent, like ruminating, re-telling your sad stories, asking disempowering questions like *What's wrong with me?* or worrying about the future.

Ruminating, or obsessive thinking, is a common and natural response in the aftermath of the breakup. We are meaning-making machines and we want to make sense of everything. It should be indulged in moderation, however, as it keeps us firmly focused on, and therefore stuck in, the past.

On the other hand, worries and anxiety keep us fixated on the future. **Between the past and the future, we hardly pay attention to the present.**

And when we do, our focus is on what's wrong or what's not working, instead of what's right and what's working.

Forgiveness

Until we have seen someone's darkness, we don't really know who they are. Until we have forgiven someone's darkness, we don't really know what love is.
– Marianne Williamson

Forgiveness – for yourself and for anyone else – is the *biggest* key to letting go, and letting go is the key to happiness and freedom after a breakup. It's also the key to living your life going forward, instead of being stuck in the past.

There are many misconceptions about forgiveness, so it's important to make sure we are clear about what it is before going on to talk about how to cultivate it.

Forgiveness is defined as an *intentional decision to release feelings of resentment toward someone who has harmed you*. Sometimes the person who has harmed you is yourself, and other times it's you who has harmed others and is asking for forgiveness from them.

It is *not* excusing or denying an offence or hurt. It's also *not* forgetting it, despite how we are told to 'forgive and forget'. It does *not* require you to reconcile with the offender or invite them back into your life.

Forgiveness is all about the forgiver. It brings the forgiver a *peace of mind.* It's not about the offender and what they deserve; it's about you and what you deserve, and you deserve to let go and move on. **It's also not letting them off the hook, but about letting yourself off the hook and clearing out more space to live the new life you truly deserve.**

How to forgive

Forgiveness is an intrinsic part of human nature, just like love. I would go a step further and say that it's hard to love without forgiveness – they go hand in hand. People whom we love *will* hurt or disappoint us. It's not a matter of if, but when (and how often!), so be prepared to forgive. *A lot.*

However, this doesn't mean that you shouldn't have any personal boundaries, and we will discuss this further in **chapter nine**. For now, just remember that forgiveness is something you do for yourself and your own peace of mind, while your boundaries are for others so they know what is not acceptable to you and what you will not tolerate.

Forgiveness is both a choice and a skill. Like any other skill you will get better at it the more you practise. At first you might find it extremely hard to forgive even the slightest wrongdoing, but it will get easier. I promise. Here are some of the best tips I have:

1. See it as something you do **for yourself**, not for anyone else

I know, I know. I sound like a broken record, but it's really *not* about your ex. It's about you and your personal power. By forgiving, the person who caused you pain no longer has power over you or the ability to drag you down to their level. Instead, you are your own boss, as you look for love, beauty and kindness all around you. You also don't become bitter and twisted from holding on to all that hate. I'm sure you've heard the saying that "happiness is your best revenge." I truly believe that.

2. Cultivate **empathy**

Consider the situation from the other person's point of view and why they would behave in such a way. Remember that at the end of the day we are humans and we all make mistakes, but they don't *define* us or the relationship. Often this is really hard to do especially immediately after the breakup or whenever the hurt is great. However, after we have regained some emotional distance weeks or months down the track, consider if we would have reacted similarly in a similar situation as our ex.

3. Throw in some **compassion**

I find this to be a game changer for me. People are doing the best they can with whatever they've got – sometimes they just have very little to work with! For example, they may be a person who is fearful or angry, closed-minded, stubborn, self-righteous, controlling, etc. "Hurt people hurt people," as they say. I know it's hard to believe, and even though they may not look it, they too feel distress and remorse. So instead of sinking to their level, we can be the bigger person.

4. Seek **peace**, not justice

Peace is separate from justice because people who hurt you may never get their just deserts (i.e. karma), but this shouldn't prevent you from moving on with your life.

Our sense of justice, or, more often, self-righteousness may be an obstacle to forgiveness. I'm always reminded of the question, "Would you rather be right or be happy?" I know what my answer is. How about you?

5. Remember that **it's a process**

Forgiveness doesn't happen in an instant. It takes time and effort, and won't come easily at first. Also, it may not result in a full release of negative feelings and that's okay. You might be able to only forgive twenty per cent for now, but it's still worth something. Next month you might be able to forgive another ten per cent and so on, until you reach a place of full forgiveness – or not. Work at your own pace and don't force it if you are not ready.

Forgiving yourself

In addition to forgiving your ex, it's time to put the stick down and stop beating yourself up for what you said or did (or didn't say or do) before, during or after your breakup or divorce. The past is in the past; no amount of self-flagellation can change it, except to cause you a whole lot of pain. Instead, we can focus on what we can control: the present and the future.

And just like forgiving others, self-forgiveness doesn't mean we let ourselves off the hook. You can forgive yourself and still believe you were at fault and have regret for what you did. It's about balancing your *personal responsibility* – taking on too much of it can be just as detrimental as not taking on enough.

By forgiving ourselves, we release destructive feelings of shame and self-blame while still experiencing *some* degree of guilt and remorse, which can be healthy and ensures that we learn our lessons and don't repeat the same mistakes from the past. In short, accept that you did the best you could at the time, and commit to acting differently in the future.

Gratitude: Thank You for the Experience

Gratitude unlocks the fullness of life. It turns what we have into enough, and more.
    – Melody Beattie

In addition to reviewing all the hard-won lessons from your heartbreak, look for the silver linings or even show gratitude for what you went through. I know, I know, this sounds like the last thing you'd want to do, but research confirms that there are many upsides to reflecting on personal benefits. I suggest that you do this by writing as it helps to crystallise your thoughts and insights.

Gratitude is a very healing emotion that can *rebalance* you, giving you a broader perspective that often gets lost due to our brain's hard-wired negativity bias or the difficulties we are going through.

A simple gratitude exercise like listing three things you are grateful for every day can sound deceptively simple – too simple to make a difference. But trust me, as someone who has done the exercise for six months straight when I went through a rough patch, it provided a gradual but powerful shift.

So be grateful for your life and what's happening in it now. It's easy to be grateful when you are in a great place in life. **The true test is to be grateful when you are *not* in a great place.**

By the way, this is the true essence of self-love – accepting not only who you are but where you are, the good, the bad and the ugly.

For example, during a breakup, you can still be grateful for what you are learning or for the compromises and sacrifices you no longer have to make.

For me, I feel enormous gratitude for the lessons my past relationships have given me so that I could reach higher for my personal and spiritual development. Each relationship takes me to the next level. As they say, "in love there is no wrong person, only a perfect teacher."

As I was reflecting on all the bad stuff I went through and the people who disappointed me, I felt grateful for them because they helped me to get to where I am today. I am the person I am today (partly) because of them, and I like who I am and where I am.

Going through heartbreak changed the trajectory of my life, career and relationships in the best way possible. I moved to different countries and cities, trained as a life coach, made new friends and started seeing a wonderful man who eventually became my husband.

At the end of the day, I don't regret anything; if I were to choose again, I would choose the exact same path. Not for the pain, of course, but for the lessons and the gifts from the experience. As I let myself be completely vulnerable for the first time in my life, I got hurt the most out of all the relationships I ever had up until then. On the flip side, I also learned the most from that breakup than *all* my previous breakups combined.

Also, love is always worth it. I wouldn't take back all the happy moments with my ex to avoid feeling the pain. I remind myself that the love was real even though the relationship wasn't meant to be.

In other words, it's a 'package deal'. We have to take the pain along with the love, the lessons and the blessings. It's not to say that we can't learn important lessons and find valuable gifts from a healthy relationship. We absolutely can. However, pain has a particular way for getting through to us. It grabs all our attention, stops us in our tracks and forces us to look at the truth like we've never done before.

And, as they say, *the truth will set you free.*

Closure

If you let go a little you will have a little peace. If you let go a lot you will have a lot of peace. If you let go completely you will have complete peace.
– Ajahn Chah

I used to believe in closures at the end of a relationship. I believed that if I were the 'dumper', I had a duty to explain why I chose to leave; and vice versa. My ex-partners and I would have some kind of big talk to find out what went wrong. And this unspoken rule seemed to have worked in my previous breakups.

As the 'dumpee' in my last relationship, I thought my ex owed me an explanation for doing what he did – cheating on me and betraying our future together. However, I learned the hard way that it wasn't meant to be.

He maintained he was innocent and told me that the three 'witnesses' I had were all lying to me. In other words, not only did he refuse to admit to cheating, but he also made me doubt others and their truthfulness. What could I expect from someone like that? I felt so fed up. I just wanted him to tell me the truth so I could move on. For a long time I agonised over the idea that I didn't have closure.

Then gradually, something shifted. I came to realise a couple of things about closure.

We want to understand, believing that understanding is all we need to move forward in our life. It's helpful but not enough; no amount of rational understanding will heal our emotional wounds. We are not purely rational beings. Our motivations are complex, and your ex – unless he or she is super self-aware – might be just as clueless as you as to why they did what they did, or what went wrong in the relationship. So you will likely end up hearing some lame excuses, rather than the truth.

More broadly, life is messy. There isn't a clear beginning, middle and ending like it is in a movie or book. So it's unlikely your relationship will be tied up in a neat bow with no messy loose ends. Realising that life (and relationships) is messy and forgiving yourself and your ex for what you did or didn't do are the quickest ways to bring closure to your life.

But the most important thing about the *illusion* of closure – and yes, it is an illusion – is that you end up giving your power away to your ex. You'll be upset if they say hurtful things. If they say something nice, you'll probably be more upset that things didn't work out! Either way, remember whatever they say is only their version of the truth, not the capital T truth.

There would have been very good reasons for your relationship to end, and you know them in your heart. Instead of judging the success or failure of your relationship based on your ex's version of the story, why not listen to your own heart and find the answer within?

In short, you do not have to expect or even demand closure from your ex – and feel stuck when they are unable or unwilling to give it to you. Use your precious energy instead to look for the lessons and blessings from your breakup and move on to the next chapter of your life.

9. Setting Boundaries

When you say 'Yes' to others, make sure you are not saying 'No' to yourself.
  – Paulo Coelho

Rocking the Boat

K nowing who we are, what we want and don't want, and then speaking up for ourselves is a life-long lesson for all.

In particular, it's a key skill that you cannot ignore in the aftermath of a breakup or divorce. There will be many occasions where you are called to speak up and ask for what you need, or to say no and set boundaries to unreasonable obligations or even threats. It's a vital part of being brave again and following your heart even more and more.

However, we may have been putting up with things and not speaking up in order to maintain peace; or maybe we have not set clear boundaries or rules from the start. This leads to a sense of low self-worth and loss of control. Our self-care is also likely to be neglected.

Why is speaking up or saying no so hard? First of all, it's important to recognise that nobody likes confrontations. It's uncomfortable, it's messy and it goes against our nature as social creatures to belong and to fit into a group.

However, the problem is even more acute for women. Society says women shouldn't offend, 'rock the boat', get angry, and so on. Also, from my experiences working with clients, many of them think that speaking up means being needy, demanding or even rude – in short, being a 'bitch'.

If we dig deeper, there is an underlying belief that may explain why: **we associate prioritising ourselves as selfish and pleasing others as selfless.**

So, rather than prioritising and expressing our needs and wants, we try to please others and make them feel comfortable at our own expense. We make either of these two biggest mistakes in our communication: not speaking up (under-expressing) or speaking up only when we are highly emotional or exploding because we have been suppressing for too long (over-expressing).

However, as discussed in **chapter six** on self-love, we need to take care of ourselves first before we can take care of others. It's not a selfish thing to do; rather, it's smart and sensible. After all, we only have so many hours in the day, and our attention and energy are limited. And yes, sometimes speaking up or saying no means you will let down others or even hurt them, but most of the time we imagine the worst.

In addition, while wanting to please another person is a beautiful thing, giving them everything they want and denying your own needs and feelings isn't. For the people-pleasers among us, there is usually a hidden fear that you will lose them if you need something different, so you compromise or even deny your own desires altogether.

The truth is that a healthy relationship has room for both of your needs. So go ahead and voice your needs because your partner isn't a mind reader. If he or she walks, it's better to know that sooner than lose yourself to someone unwilling to meet you halfway.

Alternatively, we think we can't say no in a nice way, or that there is no choice but to say yes or accept the situation as it is. No, no, no! There are ways to speak up that are neither demanding nor bitchy. In other words, it's not about what you say but *how* you say it. **And we *always* have a choice (or more). The hard truth is that we might not like the choices we have.**

For example, if our ex has insulted us or treated us disrespectfully, we have the choice to let them know they have crossed the line, and to enforce our boundaries for future interactions. We also have the choice to distance ourselves from them.

However, neither of these two choices – speaking up or cutting ties – is easy, so we avoid making the choice and just put up with being disrespected. Nevertheless, not choosing is in itself a choice, and we end up choosing long-term suffering instead of short-term discomfort.

What's really happening when you say yes to everyone else but yourself? When we say yes to others, often it means saying no to ourselves. And what happens when we constantly say no to ourselves? Each time we are sending a message to ourselves that we don't matter and our needs and values don't matter, either. So we lose ourselves, little by little, until we don't recognise ourselves anymore.

Finally, remember we are only responsible for our actions, not others' reactions. They may be offended, pleased, or may not even care. We need to give others the permission to feel however they feel, whether positive or negative. And that means allowing them to not like us. It's a hard reality that we can't please everyone.

Again, that's scary to many of us because it goes against our biological needs *and* societal expectations. We want to belong and for other people to like and accept us, and we don't want to appear to be a selfish, demanding bitch.

However, it's not our job to make other people feel comfortable. It's their job to do so. It's our job to speak our truth, in a kind and graceful way.

Instead of obsessing about how others would think or react, shift your focus back to yourself, at least for now, and see speaking up as an act of intentional self-care and a way to reconnect with your deepest needs and values.

My Story – Part II

Our job is not to deny the story, but to defy the ending – to rise strong, recognise our story, and rumble with the truth until we get to a place where we think, Yes. This is what happened. This is my truth. And I will choose how the story ends.
  – Brené Brown
  Rising Strong

So towards the end of our relationship, my ex got increasingly abusive towards me. He started calling me things like 'whore', 'shit' and many other insults. He accused me of being demanding, unreasonable and even crazy. He put me down in front of others and picked apart everything I did or didn't do.

He also accused me of cheating on him and was jealous of my male friends. I had very few male friends because I knew he was the jealous type, but somehow he still managed to get jealous. There was just no pleasing him.

Then there was the stonewalling. He would get moody without warning and would refuse to talk to me for hours or sometimes days. I felt like I was walking on eggshells all of the time.

At first, he was abusive only when he was drunk. However, soon enough he became abusive even when he wasn't. Then he started to disappear. He would come home really late at night claiming that he was at work. He got busy on weekends too – he even disappeared on me for one whole weekend, during which I had no idea where he was and my messages and calls went unanswered. Needless to say, I was a mess.

The thing was, I had never been sworn at or called such names by any boyfriend up to that point, so I was shocked and upset. I would have never put up with his erratic and selfish behaviour under normal circumstances; but I was not living under my normal circumstances – I was alone in a new country and my support system was halfway around the world.

I also felt that since I'd given up so much to be with him, I didn't want to just throw everything away. I kept secretly hoping that he was just going through a 'phase', and soon enough he would be back to the loving, passionate man that I fell in love with.

I decided to stay for three more months. During that time I would try my best to save the relationship. I didn't want to leave without doing everything I could. The regret of knowing that I could have saved the relationship would have been too great. So I reasoned and I persuaded. I begged and I pleaded (which, by the way, was a novel experience for me).

Back then I was so proud. In my earlier relationships, if things didn't seem like they were heading in the right direction, I would have just up and left. Yet, because of my ex, I was reduced to begging and pleading him to tell me what was on in his mind or why he was behaving so differently.

Nothing I did worked, of course. It was like watching a train wreck happening in front of my eyes in slow motion, and there was nothing I could do to stop it. I felt hopeless and helpless. So after trying everything I could, I finally decided to throw in the towel.

I remember it was towards the end of November. I called up my friends and acquaintances to say goodbye and to thank them for their friendships and support. It was during one of these phone calls that I found out that my ex had been cheating on me.

Apparently he had met a girl while I was away on a short family trip. He was seen hanging out with her at our apartment, cooking and eating meals together in our kitchen, and obviously sleeping in our bedroom. I can't really put into words how I felt when I first heard this, except to say that I felt a sharp, sinking sensation in my heart. It was very visceral. It was as if – all of a sudden – everything I'd held to be true had been a big, fat lie, and the ground I'd been standing on didn't exist after all.

I went to confront my ex in our apartment to hear what he had to say for himself. At first I tried to stay calm. I asked if he was cheating me. He denied it, of course. I cited the reports from my 'witnesses'. What came next really shook me, and I would never forget it. He said, "Y qué?", which meant 'So what?'

That was when I lost my cool. I slapped him in the face. He didn't like that, and things got nasty quickly. He locked my arms around my back and pushed me to the ground. I struggled and managed to stand up before I hit the ground. Then he tried to push me down again. I used all my strength to get free of his grip, but I staggered and fell backwards and hit my head against a desk.

At the time the impact didn't really register. I just remember feeling relieved to finally get free. I ran to the bedroom and locked the door behind me. Then I went to lie on the bed to catch my breath.

That was when I could feel the back of my neck getting wet. I touched it and saw my hands were covered in blood. I was stunned because I didn't really feel pain – I think I was high on adrenaline.

In panic, I called my brother – he was my go-to person whenever I found myself in trouble – and he answered immediately. Being a doctor, he was very calm, asked about my injury over the phone, assured me that it was normal to bleed a lot with a head trauma and told me to call the ambulance.

I was too embarrassed to do that, so instead I called the landlady. Luckily my ex had already fled the scene by then, so I didn't have to deal with him anymore. I waited for what felt like an eternity. Finally my landlady came and drove me to the hospital.

After we arrived at the hospital, the doctor cleaned up my wound and stitched me up. He also checked for concussion, and luckily I was cleared of that. However, I had bruises all over my arms. By the time he had finished, it was too late to go to the police. So I had to wait until the next day.

I slept really badly that night. I felt broken like a rag doll, literally and emotionally. I don't think I cried. I was still in shock. The tears came later.

I went to the police the next day. I still remember it like yesterday. It was a Tuesday. I was assigned a female caseworker and she interviewed me about what happened. I was glad that I had studied hard to improve my Spanish because it definitely came in handy, and I didn't need an interpreter. And I think being a foreigner in this instance also helped. It was so rare that they took special care of me, and things moved fast.

On the Thursday of the same week, a warrant was issued to demand my ex to be in court the next day. I didn't go back to the apartment of course after the incident. So imagine his surprise when he was served the warrant by the police. He sent me text messages accusing me of lying about the whole thing. I just turned off my phone.

Then came the big day. I went to the court with my lawyer, who was also assigned to me free of charge. I was very calm during the hearing. I think my voice broke a little at some point while giving evidence but I quickly recovered.

I remember hearing a snicker from him, obviously his way of refuting my story. Not the smartest move on his part. But he mainly kept quiet and only answered the questions from my lawyer.

I couldn't see him because we had come into the courtroom through different doors and there was a screen separating us. I remember back in my university days as a law student learning about the special setup at family courts to protect the victims of domestic violence. I just didn't think I would be a 'victim' one day.

Shortly afterwards, I left Guatemala and came back home to Australia. It took about four months for the decision to be handed down, which wasn't long at all as far as legal proceedings go.

I won the court case.

Setting Boundaries

Boundaries are about making a choice of what you will no longer tolerate from now on, then clearly communicating that choice over time. We can have different types of boundaries: physical, emotional, mental, social, sexual, etc; and they can be either big or small or anything in between.

Consider your boundaries as your defence system for your values, needs and wants. You can set these boundaries by following these tips I have adapted from a fellow life coach, Amy E. Smith.

First, **identify what areas** of your life or **with whom** you are going to establish a boundary. Be direct and try to avoid your usual automatic reaction, such as ignoring the problem, getting highly emotional or complaining about it but doing nothing.

Then, you need to decide – as clear and specific as possible – **what to do and say**. A good format could be, "I'm asking you not to _____ when _____." Decide ahead of time **when and where** you are going to deliver it. I recommend early and often, preferably when you see the same person or are in the same situation the very next time.

This way, you are less likely to rationalise away your decision or delay the conversation indefinitely. It will also help you be prepared when the situation arises again, so you can stay calm instead of reacting out of anger or frustration.

Once you've decided what to say, and when and where to say it, you then need to **actually have the conversation.** How you communicate your boundaries is just as important as the boundaries themselves, and that's with kindness. For example, you can say, "I understand your _____, but I'm also asking you to understand my _____."

Finally, you need to **enforce your boundary (or boundaries)**. This is the part where most people fail and wonder why their boundaries don't stick. Remember, your boundary may not be respected by the person with whom you set the boundary. While it's okay to give them the benefit of doubt at first, make sure you don't let the serial offenders get away. Remind them when needed, and decide when to deliver an *ultimatum*.

If and when you do deliver an ultimatum, you have to **follow it through with action**, or else it becomes an idle threat. The saying "You teach people how to treat you" should become your mantra now. For example, "If you _____, I have no choice but _____."

Then, be prepared to fight for your boundaries!

Deal breakers

Deal breakers are a specific type of boundary. They are boundaries that, if crossed, will break the relationship for you, hence the name 'deal breakers'. They are very serious and are not to be taken lightly. I would suggest starting with just one or two deal breakers – it makes communicating and enforcing them much simpler.

Typically, I have a conversation with the man I am dating at the start of our relationship to make sure that they fully understand my deal breakers and the consequences of violating them. Then I encourage them to share with me their deal breakers. This can be a bit uncomfortable, but your partner cannot know what your boundaries and deal breakers are if you don't voice them. Don't assume anything and then regret it later.

Personally, I have only two deal breakers in my relationship – violence and cheating, both of which I have zero tolerance for.

In my last relationship, I went through my deal breakers with my ex-boyfriend very early on. He was a bit taken aback and asked if I was serious when I said that I'd have no choice but to end our relationship if he cheated on me. In hindsight, that should have been a big red flag!

Unfortunately, I didn't see it at the time. In any case, nearly two years down the track, when he did cheat on me, I left him like I said I would. There was no negotiation. It wasn't easy, of course, but it was what I said I was going to do and I meant it. If I couldn't respect my own deal breakers, how could I expect him to?

Rejection

Many of us are uncomfortable with rejection, both being rejected as well as rejecting others. Learning to say no to others *and* be told no are two sides of the same coin, and it is an important skill to be able to deal with both if we want to honour our deepest needs and wants, and – yes, you guessed it – our boundaries.

When you are clear on your needs and deal breakers, it will become very easy for you to figure out whether a person is the right match for you or not. Then comes the hard part we all dread: letting them go. However, once you realise that he or she is not the right person for you, you need to communicate that clearly and respectfully at the earliest opportunity.

Yes, the conversation will be uncomfortable, hard even. And the person may react badly or be downright resentful. However, the longer you wait, the harder it is. So if you want to avoid *more* drama and resentment, do it early.

Accept the fact you will hurt their feelings. It's just a matter of time.

The sooner you tell them, the sooner they will get over their hurt and get on with their life. If you put off telling them, they will be hurt even more and resent you for 'stringing them along' and wasting their time. Not to mention you also sacrifice your own happiness the longer you stay with them.

Imagine if the situation were reversed: do you prefer that they keep dating you even though they knew you were not the right match, or do you prefer that they tell you as soon as they realised that you were not the one for them? Would you rather live a lie, or face an honest 'rejection'?

At the end of the day, a rejection is only a negative if you see it that way. You can also choose to see it as simply a lack of compatibility. Just because you are not a good match for someone else (and vice versa), it doesn't mean you are somehow less than or not enough. It just means you are not compatible.

Quite apart from the fear of rejection, some women hold on to a partner because they don't believe that they could find someone better, or is hoping they would change into someone who would be the right match.

First, you need to work on your confidence if you are worried about not finding someone better. (Read **chapter four** for tips and tools on finding courage.)

Second, a person is not a 'project'. We can certainly influence them, but changing them is another matter entirely. They will change, if they want to. No amount of cajoling or nagging will work if they don't.

10. Re-inventing Your Future

Don't settle: don't finish crappy books. If you don't like the menu, leave the restaurant. If you're not on the right path, get off it.
  – Chris Brogan

Drifting

Many women come to me for coaching after the dust has settled. Emotionally, they are no longer under the control of their hot messy feelings, and they have finished most of their paperwork and other arrangements. The fog in their heads has lifted, and instead of obsessing about the past and trying to survive the present, they are turning their attention to the future.

However, this can fill them with excitement or dread, and often it's both.

As mentioned earlier, when a relationship breaks down, not only do we lose our ex-partner, we also lose our identity as a couple, all our shared dreams and hopes for the future and even our daily routines.

This is especially true for women because our relationships play such an important role in our lives, and **we either knowingly or unknowingly give up who we are in order to be who we think we should be for our partner and our relationship**.

With the loss of our identity comes the loss of our sense of direction and purpose in life. This is no small matter, as our purpose is what drives us in life, consciously or unconsciously, and what ultimately fulfils us.

Without our goals and dreams, we feel like we are just drifting through life. Now is the perfect time to rediscover the bigger purpose that fulfils you.

In addition, going through a breakup or divorce often means that we have stopped experiencing all the small joys that we used to experience from our family, friends, interests, hobbies and even work, all of which contribute to our overall happiness and wellbeing.

This is particularly the case in a less healthy relationship where we have unwittingly made our partner the centre of our world. We have focused all our energies on making them happy and supporting their dreams in lieu of ours, so now we have to re-learn that and reclaim both our big dreams as well as our small joys.

When we have rediscovered who we are – our unique values and strengths – and what we love, then we are truly ready to re-invent our life. This involves getting crystal clear with what we want and don't want in our life, and communicating that to others. This may also include clarity around our dream partner if you are looking to date in the future.

You need to know all this before you start your next relationship. If you don't know where you are going, anywhere will take you there.

In this chapter we are going to turn our attention to re-inventing your future through setting goals and visualisations, as well as avoiding the pitfalls that prevent you from achieving your goals and visions.

Re-invention

Nobody can go back and start a new beginning, but anyone can start today and make a new ending.
– Maria Robinson

You can regain your sense of control over your future and take the necessary steps to rebuild it through two ways: planning and action.

Planning gets your focus away from the past so you stop reliving it. At the same time, it shifts the future into the present so you can take action now to re-invent a future you want. When you have a plan, every day becomes an opportunity to move toward your desired future. Best of all, it changes your life from being reactionary to full of intentions, so you can stop drifting and start living.

It's time to get clear on where you want to go. Let yourself dream. *What kind of life do you want to have? Who do you want to be? How do you want to feel?*

Write down the answers to these questions and do it for every significant area of your life – your health, your relationships, your career, and so on.

Next, make a plan. Start thinking through the steps to your new destination. *What will it take? What are your goals and milestones?*

I'll get into the nitty-gritty of goal-setting in the next section, but for now I just want to share a few quick tips and exercises to get you started on re-inventing your life. And this process doesn't have to be tedious; it can be fun and exciting too!

1. **Brainstorm** all the things you want to be, do and have in the future. Don't worry about how for now. Just dump everything onto a piece of paper. Then, circle the top three things or goals and on a separate sheet write down one of them and list three small actions you can take to make

it happen. Repeat the process for your other two goals. Then transfer your goals onto post-it notes and post them around your home or office to remind you while you take action.

Choose one goal to start with; after you finish all your small actions, you can brainstorm a few more, and so on until you reach your goal. The idea is to keep moving forward but not overwhelm yourself with long to-do lists.

2. **Create a 'breakup bucket list'.** These are the desires, hobbies or adventures you wouldn't otherwise do while you were still in your relationship. Be sure to include things that you have always wanted to try and things that make you excited. It could be big or small but ideally they should be a bit of stretch for you. Trust me, if you do this right, by the end of the exercise, you won't be able to wait to start taking action!

Similar to the first exercise, just choose one thing to start with. Put it in your calendar and do it! Then notice how you feel afterwards. Chances are you'll be feeling more alive than you've felt in a long time.

3. **Make a vision board.** Visualise your future for the next twelve months. Think about *who* you want to be and how you want to *feel*, not just what you want to do or have. You can also include visions of your dream partner: who they are, where and how you will meet them. After that, find pictures, photos or even words and quotes to represent those visions. Stick them on a big piece of cardboard and place them somewhere you can see every day. I can't stress how important it is to be surrounded by your goals and visions, so don't put them away. Otherwise it will be out of sight, out of mind!

4. Finally, don't forget to **take care of your physical appearance** as well! For sure there is inner work to be done, but the outer, fun aspect of style and beauty are important too. So get yourself a new haircut, buy some nice clothes, or join the gym and start exercising to get in

shape – whatever you need to take care of your physical appearance. Don't think it's 'shallow'. When we look good, we feel good too, even if the good feelings don't last. Happiness is as much about the moment-to-moment positive feelings as the long-term fulfilment, and they are not mutually exclusive.

I did a vision board back in 2014 shortly after I broke up with my ex, and nearly all the things on the vision board have since come true, including the chickens!

Let me explain: I put some pictures of chickens on my vision board to represent the kind of idyllic lifestyle I wanted to have, and now my husband and I live on a half-acre property and we have six chickens. How cool is that?

I was pleasantly surprised to say the least. I'd set goals before but I hadn't taken consistent action, so I didn't achieve consistent results. All I did was a simple tweak: by having my vision board and my goals list on display around our home while I took action, it made a huge difference. I have since updated my vision board and I'm excited to see what will come true next.

Goal-setting Pitfalls

If you always do what you've always done, you will always get what you've always got.
   – Anonymous

Now that you have your lists and vision board, it's time to implement your goals and visions! Despite the mountain of resources available on goal-setting, most people still fail to achieve their goals. So let me focus on the seven common mistakes people make, so you can avoid getting derailed and actually achieve your goals.

1. Being too ambitious or unrealistic

This is a biggie, and it usually means having too many goals at a time and underestimating the effort involved. Often when we want to change our lives, we want to change it completely and we want do it overnight! So we end up with a long list of goals, and become overwhelmed by the energy, time and space needed to achieve them.

When we are in our goal-setting mode, we idealise our situation and think we have unlimited energy and motivation. However, the person who has to get up at 6 am in the future to go for a run three times a week is an entirely different person. She is likely to be tired, stressed and unmotivated, rather than rested, calm and energised.

2. Not making space for the new goals

This is related to the mistake above. For example, in order to start running at 6 am three times a week, what changes or sacrifices are you going to make? What do you need to give up in order to create the space or time for this new goal (and others on your list)?

It probably means you have to go to bed at a reasonable hour, not drink too much or go out partying the night before, have a good night's sleep, remember to set your alarm clock to the new wake-up time, and so on. There are a host of new actions you have to take on in order to start the new goal of early morning runs.

Don't underestimate these small actions because each of these can become an obstacle to achieving your goals. The solution is to be prepared for all the moving pieces and to make sure you have set aside plenty of time for them, as things often take longer than you expected.

3. The goals are not specific

This is another very common mistake. Many people set a vague goal to 'get healthy', but how exactly are you going to do that?

Are you going to start exercising or going on a better diet? If it's exercising, how do you want to do it? Do you want to walk, go to the gym or play a team sport? How often and for how long do you want to do that? Once a week, three times a week, or only on the weekends? I'm sure you get my point by now.

You need to be as clear and specific about your goals as possible, so every day you wake up *you know exactly what you need to do, when and for how long*. By deciding ahead of time and committing to your decisions, there is no guessing involved and no last-minute decisions, and you can't wriggle out of your commitments. When the time comes, you just do it!

4. There are no deadlines

This is another seemingly obvious one, but sadly many people neglect it. As they say, goals are dreams with deadlines. In order to set goals instead of just daydream, you need to have deadlines. That means setting deadlines for each of your goals, as well as for the smaller milestones and actions steps.

Also, make sure you don't move your deadlines easily and often, otherwise there will be no sense of urgency. I've seen clients with the same New Year's Resolutions year in year out, because they just keep moving their deadlines. In a way, it's *worse* than not setting any goals in the first place. A goal is a promise we make to ourselves, so when we keep failing to achieve our goals, we are in fact breaking our promises and we start to doubt our ability to make the changes we want in our lives.

5. The goals are not aligned with your values and strengths

Values and strengths reflect *who you are* while goals are *what you do*, and when you do things that are aligned with who you are, they are a lot easier to accomplish. You feel energised rather than depleted by your goals, and you are more likely to feel self-motivated rather than having to push yourself all the time.

What's problematic for many people is that sometimes we have *conflicting values* and we are not aware of them, so we end up setting conflicting goals. An obvious example is that you might value family as well as financial security, so you set goals to spend more time with your family; but at the same time you also have another goal to get a promotion at work. Now something has to give!

Therefore, it helps to sit down and take a good look at your values and prioritise them. It doesn't mean you have to give up one value for another forever, but it sometimes means that you have to choose one value over another *for now*.

6. The goals are kept out of sight

It's understandable that we get excited by the goal-setting process that often after we've set our goals, we feel like we've accomplished something. It's such a shame that when we go through the sometimes arduous process of goal-setting and manage to overcome some of the common mistakes mentioned above, we then put them aside and never look at them again! We are so busy and distracted these days that the saying 'out of sight, out of mind' is truer than ever.

Your goals need to be kept at the top of your mind, and that means displaying them around your home or office as a reminder to think about them, talk to others about them and, in general, *obsess* about them to a certain extent while you work towards achieving them.

7. You are trying to do it all on your own

This is a particular problem if you are new to goal-setting. If you are a newbie, you need the support of an accountability buddy (or buddies). But even as a seasoned goal-setter, it helps to have people in your corner, especially if you haven't been getting the results you want. The buddy can either be a friend or family member, or it can also be a professional trainer, coach or mentor.

The external accountability is really powerful. Just make sure you pick a buddy who can actually hold you accountable, and can show you some tough love when you don't do what you said you were going to do.

Tell me, what is it you plan to do with your one wild and precious life?
 – Mary Oliver
 The Summer Day

11. Unstoppable Change

A year from now you may wish you had started today.
– Karen Lamb

Real Change

A quick question: how long does change take?

It takes a second, *and* it takes a lifetime.

Whenever we want to change something in our lives, be it our relationship, job or weight, it takes one second to make a decision, but then you have to follow it through with massive action, which may take months or years.

Think about it: once you've found your new love or an ideal job, or lost weight, you still have to maintain it. It's an ongoing and sometimes life-long process.

Therefore, know that your healing journey is going to be a long-term project, and that it will take a strong commitment to follow through to help you stay on course. There is a reason why they say life is a marathon, not a sprint.

When it comes to behavioural change, there are five stages: *pre-contemplation, contemplation, preparation, action* and *maintenance.* Of course, there is also relapsing. Relapsing is an important and normal part of the change process, but it's often ignored. It's where you stop or fall back into your old behaviour patterns. *Everyone* goes through it.

So, it's not about never stopping, but what you do when you stop or relapse. As long as you stay on course and don't give up, you will eventually find your new behaviours easier. Also, if later you relapse, you will be able to re-start and get back on track quickly.

Resistance

Forget all the reasons why it won't work and believe the one reason why it will.
– Anonymous

We looked at re-inventing your future in the last chapter. Planning and goal-setting allow you to have a proactive life, to get into the driver's seat and stop drifting. However, it takes more than just a plan or a road map to get from where you are now to your desired destination. You have to *act*.

This is where you have to do the hard work and when things can get messy, or messier. This is also where good old-fashioned grit and determination come in. Many people love the idea of planning but not action; they get stuck in planning, or over-planning, because that's the easy part. They are afraid that they don't have what it takes to turn their dreams into reality. So they hide behind their beautifully constructed plans of their dream future and never pull the trigger.

However, we have far more power than we think to change our life. To see this, just imagine how easy it would be to steer our lives into ruin: develop an addiction, have an affair, rack up debt, and so on. The many good things we do every day to keep our lives on track show we have great power!

If we indeed have great power, what's stopping us from putting it to work in meeting our goals? *Resistance.*

Resistance is what happens when we step outside our comfort zone to do something new or different. It shows up in different ways such as procrastination, stress, distractions (i.e. 'Shiny Object Syndrome'), or simply 'not feeling like it'.

We will look at how to take inspired action and to overcome procrastination and other forms of resistance before ending the chapter on the importance of consistency.

Drifting is easy – it takes courage to change.

Just Do It!

> *Take the first step in faith. You don't have to see the whole staircase, just take the first step.*
> – Dr Martin Luther King, Jr.

As we saw earlier in **chapter four**, the best way to overcome your fears is to be courageous. And what's the best way to be courageous? Taking action.

Taking action in spite of fear, anxiety or discomfort, and doing what you value or are passionate about is the name of the game. Remember, *nothing* happens until you take action! Waiting and hoping will get you nowhere.

One of the best ways to take action is to 'just do it!', like the Nike slogan says. (This, by the way, is one of the most brilliant marketing slogans – the word 'just' in 'Just do it!' makes taking action seem so simple and effortless.) It stops us from overthinking and overanalysing. Indeed, instead of having the habit of *action*, often we have formed the habit of *hesitation* and *overthinking*.

Just in case you are wondering about how to 'just do it', here's a quick, powerful tool – the 'Five-Second Rule'.

Mel Robbins, who introduced this deceptively simple concept, encourages you, once you have the impulse to do something, to start mentally counting down – 5 4 3 2 1 – and then physically move to start or stop an action.

Otherwise, if you let more than five seconds pass before you act, your brain will kill the impulse. It's hardwired to avoid change. In particular, the start of any change is the hardest part because of what is known as the 'initial activation energy', since change doesn't occur spontaneously and must have an initial input of energy to get started.

The Five-Second Rule is designed to put you in the driver's seat, and acts as a starting ritual that overcomes the initial activation energy required. Once you get over the initial hump, you gain momentum and can keep going.

Indeed, it's all about getting over the initial hump. Trick yourself if you have to. Make starting as easy as possible, and that's where baby steps come in. They reduce the risks of failure, and with each small success you will get an instant boost of confidence. Also, the small successes add up to build your momentum and confidence. The more you act, the more – and better – you act. Action breeds more action.

As an added bonus, taking action makes you *feel* better in the moment and in the long run. It's an instant booster of confidence for now, and it also makes you feel that you are making progress over the long term. Everyone knows that feeling whenever you have started on something that you had put off doing for a long time. The instant boost in mood and confidence is amazing!

The Magic of Scheduling

One of the most powerful things I've learned in terms of productivity is that things that get scheduled get done. So plan and schedule rather than leave anything to chance!

To make each day count, make a list of actions that are aligned with your goals or values and make sure you do one or two of them every day. If they are bigger actions, then every week or month.

Schedule them and treat them like your work appointments. Better still, make them non-negotiable; something you must do *no matter what*. You will thank yourself later.

However, make sure you fill your schedule with things that are good for your soul and you enjoy doing too, rather than just things you think you 'should' do or what others are doing. The idea is to fill your life with activities that are joyful or meaningful to you, and minimise commitments that don't bring you joy.

For example, I'm into spiritual practices, so yoga and meditation came to me naturally, and I avoid like a plague social gatherings that involve drinking and partying. But they might be exactly what you need to get out of the house!

So experiment and find what you like and spend more time doing them. I make sure I schedule at least one yoga class weekly and I also set aside time in my morning ritual to meditate. It sounds so simple, but very few people actually set aside time for their favourite activities.

Last, but not least, make time to play and do nothing too. It's okay to watch TV and play video games if they help you to relax. Just be sure to do so in moderation and don't spend hours on them each day. Research has shown that it's easy to indulge in these passive leisure activities, but they actually produce less enjoyment compared to active leisure activities such as exercising.

When in doubt, just ask yourself: *what action is consistent with the kind of person I want to be and the goals I want to achieve?*

Procrastination

Tomorrow: a mystical land where 99% of all human productivity, motivation and achievements is stored.
   – Anonymous

We can't talk about taking action without talking about its opposite: inaction or delayed action; in other words, procrastination. We all know what procrastination looks like, as most of us have a PhD in it. You've probably even noticed that it is intricately related to other forms of resistance such as stress and distractions.

The trick to overcoming resistance and taking any action is getting *started*, because we need to overcome our initial inertia (aka the 'hump'). Once you get started, the rest will flow a lot easier.

So that's the principle, and it sounds easy enough, but how do we get started?

1. Change your mindset

You will never have perfect timing or knowledge, so throw those expectations out of the window and stop waiting. It's one of the biggest mistakes to think we need to know what to do *from start to finish*. Yes, having a basic level of clarity before you start is helpful, but **the truth is that action brings clarity**, so get started as soon as you have a basic idea of what you want to achieve and what your first few steps would be.

Every action you take will bring you more clarity about your next step, and the next, until you reach your goal, or until you decide to abandon it – if you find out along the way that it's not what you need or want.

In fact, adopt an *experiential* attitude: instead of always relying on your analytical mind to think things through and analyse everything to death, get out of your head and just do it! Let your direct experiences guide and inform you as you course correct along the way.

2. Have a strong why

This means going after what you *really, really* want, not something that's nice to do or have. As we are motivated by different things, work out what motivates you. Have you ever wondered why people say they want to learn a foreign language or a musical instrument but never do? That's because it's usually just a nice, romantic idea to be able to speak Spanish or to play the guitar to wow your family, friends or a potential lover. However, there is no real passion or commitment involved.

Passion is the greatest driver and will overcome countless excuses and obstacles along the way, including your self-doubt and fear of failure. Let your desire be stronger than your fear if you haven't started on your quest; if you have started but are facing setbacks, remind yourself why you started in the first place.

Better still, reframe failure – it's just feedback, so don't take it personally. Besides, if you haven't failed, you probably haven't tried hard enough. *Success is ninety-nine per cent failure*, and all the successful people have this in common: they have failed many times. When you step outside your comfort zone, you will get scared, and from time to time you *will* fail.

3. Try developing mini habits

On a day-to-day basis, to avoid being stressed or overwhelmed, think small, very small: *what can I do today that would move me one per cent forward?* This is especially true at the beginning. Make your daily action so ridiculously small that you can't **not** do it. When the bar is set so low, it's easy to hit your target! It's all about setting yourself up for success.

For example, if you've set the goal to lose weight, aim to do one sit-up. (Isn't it ridiculously small?) Then you can gradually increase your action over time. Also, you will have great clarity – you know exactly what you need to do every day in order to move yourself toward your goals and dreams.

4. Build good support

This happens on two fronts: reducing negative influences while increasing positive ones in your life. You need to be extra careful about the naysayers or 'haters' in your life and either distance yourself from them, or fire them altogether.

At the same time, actively seek out people for support and accountability. Don't underestimate the power of accountability in getting things done. Most of us don't want to let others down, and finding accountability partners such as coaches or trainers, joining groups and classes, or being a good role model for others are all great strategies to help you stick to your goals and keep taking action forward.

They say that we are the average of the five people we spend the most time with, so who are your five people? If you can't find one single person who supports you in your existing support group, make sure you get professional support, such as a coach or a mentor.

During the last stage of my doomed relationship with my ex, I decided to run a half-marathon to distract myself from all the drama that was unfolding. However, I was under no illusion that I could do it on my own. Even though I'd been a runner for a long time, I only ran short distance (3–5 kms each time).

So I joined a running group for about three months, and we trained twice a week at some ungodly hours in the morning. I quickly discovered that some people really took running seriously. The first time I showed up for the training, I ran more than 10 kms! And no, I wasn't expecting that. (What a pleasant surprise it was, though...)

Being part of the running group made all the difference. The support and accountability of being part of the running group was awesome. After all, I didn't want to let anyone in the group down. So while my other non-runner friends were out partying late and sleeping in the next day, I got my sorry arse out of bed and trained even when I didn't feel like it.

Thanks to the training, I was able to complete the half-marathon in very good time. And, as an added bonus, I made good friends with some of my running buddies from the group. Looking back, I know the outcome would have been very different if I did it without any support.

Consistency is King

People often say that motivation doesn't last. Well, neither does bathing – that's why we recommend it daily.
– Zig Ziglar

One of the important things I've learned the hard way is that consistency is more important than intensity, and the long game is more important than the short gains. You need to do something consistently for a while before you will start to see results, and that applies to almost everything. There really are no shortcuts.

For example, they say that if you want to lose weight, it doesn't matter what diet you choose, as long as you follow it consistently. But most people don't – they either give up too soon, or they jump around from one diet to another before they see any tangible results. Then they blame it on the diet and say diets don't work.

I was no exception. Being an impatient 'grasshopper' by nature, I used to set impossible goals – finishing my assignments at the start of the school holiday, writing multiple blog posts every week, and so on – and never achieved them. Because of the seeming enormity of the goals, I would either be too scared to start, or run out of steam very quickly.

The constant 'failures' ate away at my self-esteem. **After all, a goal is a promise we make to ourselves.** So if we keep breaking our promises – never mind how crazy they are – we start believing that we are lazy, don't have the willpower or self-discipline, and worst of all **we lose trust in ourselves because we never follow through on our word.**

Now I know there is no such thing as an overnight success. As they say, "an overnight success is ten years in the making." So I have shifted my focus to the process, and to taking small actions that paved the way to bigger outcomes and transformations. And I've been so much more motivated and productive since then, while at the same time feeling less anxious and overwhelmed.

In fact, don't underestimate the power of small actions. They are like compound interest, accumulating exponentially over time to lead you to your destination faster than you think, while building your confidence and momentum along the journey. So keep plugging away with baby steps.

A few years ago I did a simple exercise of writing down three things I was grateful for every day consistently for about six months. At first I didn't see any change, but I kept at it. Then a couple of months into it, I noticed a shift. All of a sudden I wasn't just grateful for all the good things that had happened to me, but also for some of the 'bad' stuff.

Also, instead of appreciating only things that had happened in the past, I found myself starting to appreciate the things that were happening in the moment, as well as looking forward to appreciating things that were going to happen in the future. It was mind-blowing!

A word of warning, though: while it's easy to start something small, it's also easy to forget about it or to delay it indefinitely. After all, we can't really see any significant changes straight away. So it's easy to think that what we do day in day out doesn't matter. They do. They matter even more than the big milestones which come only once in a while.

Our life is made up small, seemingly mundane moments and it's up to us how we want to live them. As someone wise once said, how we spend our days is how we spend our lives, and if we take care of the moments, the years will take care of themselves.

12. New Hope Map

Joy is what happens to us when we allow ourselves to recognise how good things really are.
Marianne Williamson

Love Your Journey

N ow we've come to the very last stage of our healing process.

This is where acceptance occurs. Don't worry if you are not here yet; you can come back to this chapter later. And I promise you will get here.

Before I go on and talk about acceptance, finding meaning and the idea of upturn or falling forward, I want to mention the importance of fun and joy.

Most people dread the healing process and can't wait to get to the 'destination' where they feel like they are back on their feet again. But as you know now, healing takes time – from a few months to a few years, depending on the circumstances of the breakup and how fast or slow you process it and change.

So, you might as well try your best to enjoy the journey, instead of making it – and yourself – miserable the whole time. Try to incorporate some fun and play into your life at this stage of your healing journey. In fact, the earlier you can reconnect with your inner child, the better. You don't have to wait for anyone's permission or for things to get better. Having more fun and play in your life helps you to heal in the first place.

Some great questions you can ask yourself now are:

- *Is there a part of me that I have lost connection with (and can now reconnect with)?*
- *Was there something – hobbies, passions, pastimes – I used to enjoy that I've forgotten or given up?*

Don't underestimate how much fun and joy a hobby, passion or connection can give you when you bring back just a small piece of it into your life. If you don't have anything from your past, now is the perfect time to try something new.

Reclaiming old passions and having new adventures not only allow you to rebuild your sense of identity independent of your ex, they also distance you from potential triggers that can bring up old memories with him or her.

Acceptance, Meaning, Upturn

When the heart grieves over what it has lost, the spirit rejoices over what it has left.
  – Sufi Proverb

Acceptance

Let's take a look now at the final phase of the three post-breakup phases I described in **chapter one**: acceptance.

It's a word we hear a lot, especially in the personal development world. But it is one of those abstract words that are hard to define and can mean very different things to different people. And it seems so elusive. For me, *acceptance is being with what is, exactly as it is.*

There are times in life we may not be able to change our circumstances despite our best efforts, and we need to accept things as they are. Breakups are one of such times. We accept our pain, we accept our anger, and we even accept our lack of acceptance. It's at the end of the grief cycle, but not everyone gets there.

There are a lot of misconceptions about acceptance. Many people think that if you accept something, it means you have to like it or that you are okay with it. It doesn't mean that at all. You can accept things or situations as they are and *not* like them.

It simply means that you are no longer in the denial stage of the grief process wishing that things *should* be different, and you've now moved on to the acceptance stage where you are seeing and feeling things clearly and fully.

Also, acceptance is not about giving up or resignation. It's the opposite. It's about embracing the truth as we know it – no more and no less. We don't exaggerate our suffering or downplay it, nor do we ruminate or wallow in it. It's about engaging with emotions, in particular negative emotions, thereby reducing them. All of this takes a lot of effort and courage, so it's most definitely not about giving up.

The goal of acceptance, however, is *not* to reduce negative feelings but rather to change our relationship with them by engaging with *all* emotional experiences – positive and negative – in a non-judgmental, self-loving way. Instead of denial and resistance, there is a feeling of ease and spaciousness.

Like I said, acceptance is elusive – it is one of the hardest things in life, and also one of the most valuable.

Finding meaning

I don't think of all the misery but of the beauty that still remains.
  – Anne Frank
  The Diary of a Young Girl

It's not always easy to see beyond the pain for the meaning and lessons of your breakup experience. However, it is an essential part of the healing process. First of all, it's simply about being smart and avoiding repeating the same mistakes again.

As Einstein famously said, "insanity is doing the same thing over and over again and expecting different results." We want to focus on doing things differently, as what we were doing didn't work.

Having said that, finding the reason (or reasons) for the breakdown of your relationship consists of only the small story. There is a bigger story or learning behind it.

So what have you learned? A lesson in dealing with rejection or betrayal? Lack of self-worth and self-love? Vulnerability and trust? Standing up for yourself and setting boundaries?

Like a gold mine, there is so much to be learned, if you are willing to pause and dig deep instead of moving on with your life quickly.

For example, here is a summary of some of the valuable lessons I learned from my breakup, ranging from the practical to the more spiritual.

- *Noticing warning signs and red flags of a failing relationship* and in particular of infidelity, while at the same time finding a balance between awareness and paranoia.
- *How to be in a committed relationship without losing myself* (see **chapter six**). I had wanted to know the answer to this dilemma for as long as I could remember, and finally I got clarity. Radical self-love and self-care were the key.
- *Not putting my life on hold, and the importance of staying physically active and pursuing personal goals* (see **chapters 10 and 11**). In fact, they can provide a healthy outlet for your relationship woes. While my relationship was falling apart, I trained for a half-marathon and studied for my DELE level C1 exam in Spanish (the second highest level of Spanish competency exam that a non-native language speaker can sit for), both of which I aced.

- *The importance of friendships* – especially with other women – *and staying socially engaged* in general rather than hiding and isolating myself (see **chapter seven**).

- *Standing up for myself, defining and defending my values* (see **chapter nine**) Closely related to this is setting *and* reinforcing boundaries. Instead of respecting them, some people will try to challenge your values or push your boundaries to see how serious you are. This in itself can be a red flag!

- *Knowing my absolute limits – what I would or would not do for love* (see **chapter nine**). I became *crystal clear* on my deal breakers and how far I would go to save a relationship before calling it quits.

- *Love is not enough.* Here I'm referring to love from someone outside us. It is essential but not sufficient for a relationship to survive. I already knew this, but I had to be reminded again.

- *Knowing when to stay and when to walk away, and having the courage to do so* (see **chapter four**). Many of us stay too long in a relationship. Hope is a double-edged sword: it helps us to work through relationship bumps, but we also wait too long for things or the other person to change.

Upturn: failing forward

The world breaks everyone and afterward many are strong in the broken places.
  – Ernest Hemingway
  A Farewell to Arms

Most people have heard of post-traumatic stress disorder (PTSD), but what's less known is **post-traumatic growth (PTG)**. In the wake of trauma, not everyone will develop anxiety or a mental health problem. Instead, some will experience the positive personal changes of PTG.

While PTSD features regularly in the media, it is relatively rare in reality. Only a small percentage of people cannot function the way they used to after a traumatic event; the majority finds that they've gained something from their ordeal and have experienced PTG.

PTG is more than just resilience or bouncing back; it is bouncing *forward*, or bouncing higher than before. Even though intuitively we know that we grow stronger from adversity such as a breakup or divorce, we focus our attention mostly on the trauma itself, forgetting all the blessings in disguise.

By the way, I am not saying that adversity itself is a good thing – far from it! The process of growth does not reduce the pain of loss and heartbreak. What I'm saying is that out of loss there is often gain, and a crisis can often transform people in positive ways – they become stronger, wiser and more compassionate. So if it's there, use it, but don't seek it out!

In any case, the research on PTG provides powerful proof that as humans *we're wired to grow as a result of hardship*. Therefore, it radically changes our ideas about trauma and how it inevitably leads to a dysfunctional life. **We might be bruised and battered for now, but we are never broken.**

Celebrate Singleness

Often we don't read about being single in a relationship or dating book. Even less, celebrate it. Most people – and their family and friends – seem to assume that they will eventually get into another committed relationship.

However, the reality is that today one in three women in Australia aged between 30 and 40 are single, while one in four Australians live alone. Living alone is more common for older people, and particularly for women. More than one in three women aged 65 years and older live by themselves.

Therefore, it's important to think about the likelihood that you will be single – possibly for the rest of your life – after your breakup. Some women find this prospect frightening. This is understandable. It's in our DNA to want to belong and be part of a group. Loneliness is hard to bear, especially for a long period of time. It can also provoke FOMO (Fear Of Missing Out), as you feel anxious that you are missing out on opportunities. This is particularly true if you expected to start a family with your ex but now find yourself unexpectedly single again.

Also, things could be hard internally when you are single because all of a sudden the 'spotlight' is on you. Previously you might have all your attention on your ex, especially if you were in a less healthy relationship, hiding behind their needs and wants. Now you've shifted it back on yourself: it's exciting but also terrifying at the same time, just as you would feel if you were standing in the spotlight.

On the one hand, you don't have to make any compromises in order to please your partner or to not 'rock the boat'. On the other hand, however, with freedom comes responsibility, so now it's up to you to make all the decisions and to take care of yourself physically, emotionally and financially. And that can be scary if you are not used to that level of freedom and responsibility.

First of all, it's important to remember that being single doesn't mean that you are missing out. There are as many upsides to being single as there are in a relationship, but if you only focus on the downsides, you'll find only the downsides.

Indeed, the grass isn't greener elsewhere. You'd be surprised at the number of people who are in dead-end relationships and would be a lot happier if they had left. We are so afraid of being alone that we put up with being unhappy or even disrespected in a relationship.

The reality, however, is you end up feeling alone anyway if you are in a unhealthy relationship where there is little or no real intimacy and communication. So don't envy anyone. Instead, make the best of your situation while you are single and know that your time will come, if you choose to be with someone.

When you are on your own, take the time to know yourself, love yourself and do all of the things you had less time for when you were in a relationship – friendships, career, hobbies, travelling, or even just relaxing and sleeping in. Find your tribe of singles so you don't feel so alone in a culture that still considers couples as the norm.

More deeply, however, having someone else love you doesn't rescue you from the homework of loving yourself. Being single, at least for a while, allows you to shift your focus back on yourself and stop looking outside yourself for someone or something to make you feel better. As we discussed in **chapter six** on self-love, the only love that will actually heal the pain in the long run is your own. So give it to yourself!

Also, by rebuilding a strong sense of identity, self-confidence and self-love, and removing the barriers in the way, you will arrive at a point where you feel whole and complete in yourself. Don't buy into the popular belief that you need somebody else to 'complete' you or to fill a void. Think of a potential partner as somebody who could complement you, but without them you would still be perfectly okay.

In fact, more than okay, because nothing is missing and nothing needs to be fixed. After all, you don't need to fix something that's not broken.

I have had similar fears after my own blindsiding breakup. I thought I messed up, was broken for good, and would be on my own forever. Luckily after doing the intense inner work, I gradually rebuilt my identity and restored my self-confidence.

I felt whole and complete in myself, and I knew I would be ok even if I stayed single forever. I could love and take good care of myself and meet my own needs, and I didn't have to wait for someone else to come along to do that. In my mind, it would be a bonus if and when I met a wonderful man, but it wasn't a necessity.

It was such a radical shift! It gave me freedom and a sense of peace – freedom to choose to stay single or get into another relationship, and peace from knowing that either way I would be fine.

Since I felt whole and complete in myself, and that nothing was missing or needed fixing, I wasn't in a hurry to get back to dating. When I eventually did, I made sure that I was upfront about my needs and wants. For example, I was really clear right from the start that I wanted to have children, and I took my time getting to know the men I was dating.

Going into the dating scene with an attitude of wholeness and self-sufficiency allows you to attract men who are on a similar wavelength. That is, they admire women who are self-assured and authentic. Of course it can be a turn-off for other men who are looking for someone to 'rescue' or with whom to be in a co-dependent relationship. But that's great news, because we want to repel those men anyway!

Dating with Confidence

Every heartbreak brings you one step closer to being with the person you are meant to be with.
   – Anonymous

This book is not meant to be about dating, so I will be brief and offer a few key pointers and reminders if you find yourself wanting to date again.

Stay open

It's hard to keep your heart open after we've been through a difficult breakup; we want to protect our heart from being hurt again. However, it's the price we pay for living a full, wholehearted life, not a half-hearted one. Indeed, instead of retreating from life and from love, a shocking loss may be a great opportunity to break your heart open and to expand your life and your capacity to love yourself and others.

Nonetheless, I'm not asking you to just drop all of your defences and make yourself dangerously vulnerable. We all need and deserve protection.

At the same time, while you cannot avoid getting hurt, you may be able to minimise it. One of the best ways I know how is to cultivate clarity and be intentional about your search, and designing your ideal partner is a great way to get you started.

This way, you are not relying on blind luck or playing a numbers game, as many dating 'experts' seem to suggest. Instead, you are being smart and attracting only suitable candidates and repelling the undesirable ones, thereby saving your precious time, energy and tears.

Design your ideal partner

The more specific you are about what you want, the better, as you will be able to spot the potential candidates quickly.

Do you know the qualities that a man has to have to meet your deepest emotional needs and wants? And what are your deepest emotional needs and wants for that matter? Be really honest with yourself. For example, if financial security is important to you, say so. Don't feel like you have to go for a guy who is not financially stable, even if he has a great personality.

Also, include your deal breakers so you won't repeat the same mistakes or patterns from your past relationships. We all know friends or acquaintances – or even ourselves – who keep attracting men just like their ex. By deliberately designing your ideal partner, you choose a new future instead of repeating the same past over and over again.

Be proactive

This may sound really obvious, but if you've decided that you want to date instead of staying single, then you need to be proactive. It's not about waiting passively. There are so many things you could do right now while you are single, so take the time to know yourself, love yourself and do the inner work necessary.

In particular, build up your self-love and self-worth. The most breathtaking love may come into your life, but if you don't feel worthy you won't be able to receive it. Also, if you are lacking in self-love, you will be seeking love from outside with neediness and desperation to fill a void that only you can fill with unconditional love toward yourself.

In short, aim to become your best self for when that person comes along. Instead of trying to find the right partner, focus on *being* the right partner.

Experiment and evolve

Sometimes, after years of being in a relationship and doing everything we can to please our ex-partner, we forget who we are and what we truly want (or don't want), so we need to re-learn that. And that means you will need to experiment.

Dating helps you do just that. It helps you learn what you like and don't like, or want and don't want from a relationship. It's a learning experience, and like any learning experience you will make mistakes and sometimes hit dead-ends, but it doesn't mean it wasn't worth it. Every person and every relationship teaches us something valuable. That's why they say it's better to have loved and lost than not loved at all.

As you grow, the people you date or partner with should reflect that and be better than the ones before. Each person becomes the mirror to reflect everything about you right back. And just when you think you have everything worked out and under control, the next layer is revealed.

As your relationships get better, in turn you get better too. You will continue to grow and evolve as your relationships continue to grow and evolve with you.

Never settle

I can't stress this enough, but *never, ever settle*. I know it can get lonely sometimes, but you will be wasting your time and doing yourself an injustice. Don't let a momentary lapse of judgment or slump in self-worth determine your choice. Instead, stay on your own side, remind yourself of your worth and be selective.

After all, as I like to remind my clients, there are a lot of people out there! In fact, seven billion of them to be more exact. Even if the person you are looking for is one in a million, do you know how many potential partners you will be looking at? 7,000!

The odds are in your favour. You will find that someone.

Afterword: The End = The Beginning

When we deny the story, it defines us. When we own the story, we can write a brave new ending.
   – Brené Brown

Thank You

Thank you for making it this far. I have written this book for people like you who are going or have been through a heartbreak and are trying to find their way back to themselves. Thank you for your courage, for showing up and for being willing to shift and change.

This is where our journey together ends. This is also where your own journey starts. You may want to start implementing what you've learned straight away, or you may want to go back and review certain sections of this book first. *Whatever you do, don't just put the book aside and forget about it!*

At the same time, don't feel like you have to implement everything all at once. Just start with one strategy or tool that really stood out for you. Focus on incorporating it into your life, and when you feel like you have a solid handle on that, then start adding another. You don't want to get overwhelmed. As we've seen in the book, *overwhelmed = inaction.*

Even if you only implement one thing from this book and it changes your life for the better in some small way, this book will have served its purpose.

Indeed, small actions, like compound interest, lead to big results if you give them enough time to work their magic. Consistency is more important than intensity over the long run. After all, life is a marathon, not a sprint.

Simple, consistent action will change your life. You don't need advanced, fancy moves most of the time. Besides, once you've mastered the fundamentals, everything else becomes easier.

Forgetting and Remembering

We already have everything we need. There is no need for self-improvement. All these trips that we lay on ourselves – the heavy-duty fearing that we're bad and hoping that we're good, the identities that we so dearly cling to, the rage, the jealousy and the addictions of all kinds – never touch our basic wealth. They are like clouds that temporarily block the sun. But all the time our warmth and brilliance are right here. This is who we really are. We are one blink of an eye away from being fully awake.
– Pema Chödrön
Start Where You Are

A lot of personal development, especially if you have been immersed in it for a while, is about reminding us of what we already knew inside us but forgot along the way.

That said, often we need to be reminded of something over and over again until it really sinks in and becomes part of our lifestyle or even part of our identity. *We remember, we forget, and then we remember again.*

So if you think you will forget or get distracted because of how busy you are and all the 'noise' around you, find a way to remind yourself.

Set up a system of reminders and rewards for staying on track by keeping what you want at the top of your mind. They don't have to be complicated. In fact, keep them as simple as possible – for example, schedule them in your calendar or set phone reminders.

Apart from reminders, set yourself up for success in other ways with structures, systems and supports. Do whatever it takes to make things work *for* you. Don't just rely on your precious willpower, or on beating yourself up because you think it will motivate you to change. Engage in personal or professional support to help keep you accountable.

Keep Showing Up

Don't wait for miracles. Your whole life is a miracle.
– Albert Einstein

If you've read this far, I'm sure you are interested in sustainable growth, not in one-off flukes. You have been on your way to becoming who you have the potential to, so don't stop. Finish what you started.

Sometimes it will feel hard; we'll come up against resistance and other blocks. From time to time we'll also fall off the track.

Don't beat yourself up. Just keep showing up anyway. *Over and over again.*

A Happy Ending

My story is no fairytale, but it does have a happy ending.

I'm now married to a wonderful and loving man, who is also really smart and sexy. And he makes me laugh. We have a beautiful little baby girl. What more could a girl want?

I couldn't have imagined myself in this place when I broke up with my ex-boyfriend. In fact, as I mentioned before, I was convinced that I would never find someone better. My friends were trying to tell me there were plenty of fish out there and I would love again, but I didn't believe them. I didn't care if there were plenty of fish out there – I just wanted one fish, and that was my ex. It was crazy, and I was so wrong!

I know it's unfair to compare, but I'm going to do it anyway – my husband is 10, no, 100 times better than my ex. For starters, he is a man, not a boy pretending to be a man. And did I mention that he is also really smart, sexy and funny?

By the way, he probably won't read this book, so I'm not saying any of this to make him happy. I'm living proof that life is full of possibilities and you can turn your heartbreak into a breakthrough. Just when you think that you've hit a dead-end and all the doors have closed on you, there are in fact other doors waiting for you to open.

So don't lose hope or focus on the closed doors; try something different instead today.

Tools for Your Journey

It is never too late to be what you might have been.
  – Anonymous

We are all on a journey somewhere, but we don't have to travel alone. Here are some ways that I can support you going forward on your journey.

'Love Your Journey'

This is my virtual home where I share thoughts on a host of topics from self-compassion to mindfulness, including healing a broken heart. To explore more, visit www.loveyourjourney.net.

'Women Choosing Their Journey' Meetup

When I was grieving the loss of my relationship, I wanted to connect with other women who were going through a similar situation, but I couldn't find them.

So I promised myself that when I was better I would create a support group for women facing difficult transitions, and this was the result.

Visit

www.facebook.com/groups/womenchoosingjourney/
www.meetup.com/WomenChoosingTheirJourneyBrisbane/

Coaching Programs

Confidence & Happiness Booster

- Boost your happiness in the moment
- Be more loving and kind towards yourself
- Let go of perfection and release judgment
- Build your self-belief and confidence
- Establish a positive and resilient mindset
- Build a strong support network around you

Life Purpose Breakthrough

- Find clarity in your personal or professional direction
- Understand your unique values and strengths
- Develop a vision for your life or career/ business
- Create exciting yet achievable goals to achieve your vision
- Get unstuck, stop procrastinating and start moving forward
- Create consistent results through mindful action
- At the same time, enjoy your journey more
- Make your life more purposeful and meaningful
- Feel proud of yourself and your achievements
- Be the person you have always wanted to be

Your New Life Program

As the name suggests, this program helps you to create your new life and a brand new you! In this program, we cover the topics in the Booster and Breakthrough programs, but we go a lot deeper. There is also more one-on-one coaching in this program to give you all the support you need.

About the Author

A nnie Huang is no stranger to major life transitions, as she knows the challenges intimately. Having lived in four different countries, she had also worked both within and outside the legal profession in various capacities. Being flexible and resilient, she had always managed to re-invent herself successfully at each turn.

She was born and raised in Taiwan. She moved to Sydney, Australia with her family at the age of 14. She didn't speak English and was extremely shy, so she found it challenging in the first couple of years to fit into the new country and culture. Eventually she found her groove and went on to study law in university, eventually becoming a lawyer.

After working as a refugee advocate, she got her dream job in her early 30s working for the United Nations, where she fought against human trafficking. Then she met a man whom she thought was 'the one'. She quit her job and moved to Central America to be with him. However, the relationship broke down after nearly two years when she found out that he was cheating on her.

She came back to Australia heartbroken and jobless, totally lost and not knowing what to do with her life. On top of that, she had moved to a new city rather than going back to Sydney. She hit rock bottom and felt lost, overwhelmed and utterly alone in the world.

Luckily for her, she found life coaching and learned valuable tools and strategies to heal herself and get back on her feet again. After finishing her training, she started coaching other women through their major life transitions and heartaches in her new adopted city, Brisbane, and abroad. She also started her own Meetup group to provide support to women in difficult transitions so they didn't have to go through what she went through alone.

Annie has a Bachelor of Laws (LLB) and Master of Laws (LLM) and is a solicitor in NSW. After transitioning into life coaching, she is now an Associate Certified Coach (ACC) through the International Coach Federation (ICF). She is also a certified Wellness Inventory Coach. She has coached people all over the globe from Australia, USA, UK, Italy, China and the UAE.

To find out more, visit Annie's website

www.loveyourjourney.net

or contact her at

annie@loveyourjourney.net.

Love Your Journey

Thank you for being a part of this journey with me. If you are interested in working together, I offer:

1. Breakup to Breakthrough Call

Apply for Your FREE 60-Minute *Breakup To Breakthrough Call* to Create a Crystal Clear Vision of Your NEW Life and Start Making That Vision Your New Reality.

During the call, we will:

1. Create a crystal clear vision of the life you want to have, the people you want to surround yourself with, and the practical steps you can take straight away to start making that vision your new reality.

2. Uncover hidden ideas or beliefs that could be sabotaging your progress in letting go of the past and moving on from your breakup, separation or divorce.

3. Leave the session renewed, re-energised, and inspired so that you are ready to jumpstart the next chapter of your life.

To apply, visit www.loveyourjourney.net/breakthrough-call/

2. Women Choosing Their Journey Meetup

This is a group for women facing difficult transitions and heartbreaks. We are a super friendly bunch and you will find the support, connection and inspiration you are looking for here!

To learn more and to join online, visit

www.facebook.com/groups/womenchoosingjourney/

If you live in Brisbane, come to our monthly Meetups!

www.meetup.com/WomenChoosingTheirJourneyBrisbane/

3. Coaching Programs and Workshops

I run regular coaching programs and workshops as well as one-on-one coaching sessions.

Confidence & Happiness Booster

Life Purpose Breakthrough

Your New Life Program

½ Day Goal-setting Workshop for Women

½ Day Self-love Workshop for Women

½ Day Overcoming Inner Critic Workshop for Women

To find out more, call me on 0410747863 or email me at annie@ loveyourjourney.net.

CPSIA information can be obtained
at www.ICGtesting.com
Printed in the USA
BVHW030639220321
603169BV00008B/830